ACTIVATE YOUR IMPACT

Activate Your Impact

A Guide to Living Out Loud in Business, Life and Faith

Brooke Thomas

©2025 All Rights Reserved. No portion of this book may be reproduced, stored in a retrieval system, or transmitted in any form or by any means—electronic, mechanical, photocopy, recording, scanning, or other—except for brief quotations in critical reviews or articles without the prior permission of the author.

Published by Game Changer Publishing

Paperback ISBN: 978-1-967424-10-8

Hardcover ISBN: 978-1-967424-11-5

Digital ISBN: 978-1-967424-12-2

www.GameChangerPublishing.com

DEDICATION

To my daughters Reagan and Riley,

Everything I do—every word I speak, every woman I encourage, and every impact I make—is with you in mind. You are my legacy, my greatest calling, and my reminder that the work we do today isn't just for us, but for the next generation.

This book is for you and for every daughter—born and yet to be born—who will rise with boldness, lead with purpose, and Live Out Loud. May you always know the power of your voice, the strength of your faith, and the responsibility we carry to activate the impact God has placed within us.

With all my love,
Mom

READ THIS FIRST

Just to say thank you for reading Activate Your Impact, I've put together three exclusive bonuses to help you lead boldly and live out your calling. When you scan the QR code, you'll get instant access to Activate Your Breakthrough—a 3-part video challenge to clarify your vision, release what's holding you back, and take bold action. You'll also unlock a Biblical Leadership Style Quiz to discover how God uniquely designed you to lead, plus 30 powerful prayers to speak over your business, leadership, and life. I can't wait to see how you activate what God has already placed in you!

Scan the QR Code Here:

ACTIVATE YOUR IMPACT

A GUIDE TO LIVING OUT LOUD IN BUSINESS, LIFE AND FAITH

BROOKE THOMAS

Praise For

ACTIVATE YOUR IMPACT

"There is no one more qualified to help you activate your impact than Brooke Thomas. She has a unique ability to see and call out the potential in every person. Her passion and wisdom will help you step up and into your purpose."

—Christine Caine
Founder A21 & Propel Women

"Brooke Thomas is a force for good and a force for love in this world. She's the real deal, and that's rare!"

—Jamie Kern Lima
Host of The Jamie Kern Lima Show podcast,
New York Times bestselling author of *Worthy*
and *Believe It*, Founder, IT Cosmetics

"Being around Brooke activates something in you—her passion, purpose, and presence are undeniable. She leads with conviction and calls others higher. She's a true leader, and this book is a powerful extension of that calling."

—Dr. Josh Axe
NYT Best Seller and Host of *The Dr. Axe Show*

We all were born for a purpose, it's up to us to figure out what that is. Sometimes we need permission to be the bold unapologetic leaders we were born to be. This inspirational book not only helped me zero in on what my next chapter can look like but it also gave me a new perspective on how to activate my impact in a way that is uniquely me.

—Cheryl "Salt" James
of the iconic hip-hop duo Salt-N-Pepa

"There are women who cheer you on from the sidelines, and then there are women who walk beside you and speak your name in every room that matters. Brooke is that kind of woman—a magnetic force for connection, growth, and unwavering purpose. Her devotion to helping women rise into their power is the kind of leadership this world needs more of. Activate Your Impact is a soulful call to action—for every woman who's ready to align her faith with her fire."

—Hayley Paige
Wedding Dress Designer and Creative director
at SHE IS CHEVAL, Founder of A GIRL
YOU MIGHT KNOW FOUNDATION

"Brooke Thomas is a Kingdom-minded powerhouse. Her leadership is Spirit-led, her wisdom is time-tested, and her heart for activating women in business and faith is unmatched. She leads with excellence, humility, and bold obedience—and the fruit of her life speaks volumes."

—Kathryn Gordon
CEO of The Jon Gordon Companies,
Founder of Gordon Publishing and
Bestselling Author of *Relationship GRIT*

"Brooke Thomas is a powerhouse of purpose and faith. In *Activate Your Impact*, she gives you the blueprint to step boldly into who God created you to be. Her passion is contagious, and her impact is real— I've seen her help countless women rise, lead, and live activated. This book will inspire you, challenge you, and launch you into your calling."

—Morgan Kline
CEO & Co-Founder of Burn Boot Camp

"Brooke Thomas is a powerhouse for the kingdom of God. Her Spirit-led business acumen is exceptional and contagious. Watching her inspire, equip, and launch women into their callings has been incredible to witness. She is the real deal. A queen maker and a leaders leader. This is a must-read for anyone desiring to swing for a God home run in business and life."

—Pastor Mark Francey, Oceans Church

"Brooke Thomas is one of the most powerful spiritual leaders of this generation. She leads with faith, kindness and courage, and can genuinely shift your path with her teachings.

Activate Your Impact is one of those books that will change you for good. It's the kind of book you want to share with the people you love most in life."

—Myka Meier
Founder Beaumont Etiquette,
2xs Best Selling Author of
Modern Etiquette Made Easy

"Brooke Thomas is a catalytic voice for this generation. Her bold faith, strategic mind, and passion for activating women in their God-given calling is contagious. She doesn't just speak about impact—she lives it every day."

—Pastor Rachelle Francey
Oceans Church and
Host of *Collective Talk* podcast

"A powerful, prophetic manual that will activate your purpose and breathe life into your future. This is a must-read for the visionary leader who is ready to go all in, bring massive impact to the marketplace, and glorify the kingdom of God."

—Rachel Luna
Award-Winning Author of
*Permission to Offend: The Compassionate
Guide for Living Unfiltered & Unafraid*

"Brooke Thomas is a faith-fueled force. Her passion for celebrating and elevating women is contagious. Brooke's character and authenticity shine through everything she does. Activate Your Impact is a book written to lead you into taking action to boldly live out your God-given calling. This book is the foundation for women ready to rise, lead, and walk fully in their purpose."

—Jesse Ewell
Creator-Coach of Habit Based Lifestyle

"Activate Your Impact" is a blueprint for women who are ready to rise in purpose and power. If you know you were meant for more, this is the book that will push you over the edge. Brooke brings truth, strategy, and scripture together in a way that feels both practical and prophetic."

— Tresa Todd
Founder of the Women's Real Estate Investors Network.

"If you've ever been in a room with Brooke Thomas, you have experienced what activation feels like. Her passion for life is contagious. Her faith, fire, and focus create a ripple effect wherever she goes. She has personally helped me activate a dream that had been in my heart for a long time. She is a leader for leaders - and this book will unlock the leader inside of you and the dreams that are buried in your heart."

—Alex Seeley
Co-founder of The Belonging Co Church
and Author of *Tailor Made*

"Activate Your Impact is more than a book—it's a blueprint for women who are ready to fully step into their Kingdom purpose and divine authority. Brooke brings Scripture, strategy, and story together in a way that feels both practical and prophetic. Her message is right on time!"

—Meredith Andrews
Worship Leader/Songwriter/Recording Artist
with CURB Records

"Brooke Thomas is one of our nation's leading voices to empower the destinies of women. I am amazed at how she consistently champions other women, tearing down competition, raising the standard of character development, strengthening trust in God, and cultivating long-term friendship in community."

—Jenny Donnelly
Founder, Her Voice Movement
#DontMessWithOurKids-USA

CONTENTS

Introduction ... 1

SECTION 1: BUSINESS

1. Activate Your Purpose ... 13
2. Activate Your Creativity ... 31
3. Activate Your Confidence ... 43
4. Activate Your Vision ... 59

SECTION 2: LIFE

5. Activate Your Capacity ... 77
6. Activate Your Relationships ... 93
7. Activate Your Legacy ... 115
8. Activate Your Peace ... 131

SECTION 3: FAITH

9. Activate Surrender ... 145
10. Activate Your Belief ... 163
11. Activate Your Obedience ... 179
12. Activate Your Worship ... 197

The Activation Is Yours ... 211
Want More? ... 215
Connect With Brooke ... 217
Partner in Impact ... 219
Acknowledgments ... 221
About Brooke Thomas ... 225

INTRODUCTION

Your life is a GIFT from God to the world.

Does that thought make your spirit rise up in agreement, shouting, "Yes! I know it!"—or does something inside you shrink, whispering, "That can't be for me ..."?

If the weight of past failures, doubts, or disappointments makes it hard to fully receive, then you've come to the right place.

When you embrace this truth and know that your life was divinely designed with purpose, you will step into a new level of freedom. You will wake up and come fully alive. And you will walk boldly in everything God has destined you to BE and DO.

But what's holding you back? What's stopping you from showing up as the fullest, most powerful version of yourself?

Is it the lies you've been telling yourself? The forgiveness you haven't been able to release? The false labels you've been holding onto?

You don't have to carry any of it anymore. Your Creator—your Heavenly Father—fully sees and loves you. Isn't that what we all desire in life? To be fully seen and fully loved for who we are?

Before I ever had the opportunity to lead teams of hundreds of thousands across the globe and mentor women building multimillion-dollar businesses, I was battling my own doubts. I spent years wondering if I was really capable of creating impact.

Despite rising to the highest level of two successful network marketing companies and making over 100 million in sales, it wasn't the achievements or accolades that gave me confidence—it was the realization that my worth was never tied to my success. It was anchored in God's purpose for me.

My greatest passion is to help you become all that you were born to be. I have an URGENCY for you to walk out God's calling on your life!

We are meant to live fully awake. But it's easy to drift into autopilot, sleepwalking through the days without realizing it.

Little by little, your confidence shrinks. You may not even notice it at first. Maybe someone or something clouds your vision. You feel stuck. Incapable. But you are capable! Whatever "that thing" is that is keeping you small, I want to show you how to surrender it to God so you can create space for something BIGGER.

It's time to awaken to **ACTIVATE YOUR IMPACT!**

The truth is, you already have everything you need. But sometimes, it takes a moment that shakes you or a challenge that tests you to fully realize the strength and purpose God has placed inside you.

THE MOMENT THAT ALMOST STOLE MY IMPACT

I remember walking into what I thought was a routine check-up. I was 26 years old, newly married, and pregnant. Expecting nothing more than a quick appointment.

But then, they sent me to oncology.

"Oncology?" I asked. "Why oncology?"

The doctor looked at me solemnly. "According to the severity of your bloodwork, we are here to tell you that you have stage 3 cancer. It's melanoma. When you're pregnant, skin cancer spreads hard and fast because of your hormones."

In that moment, everything around me blurred. My heart pounded. My mind raced. *Cancer? Stage 3?* This couldn't be happening.

Then came the recommendations: immediate chemotherapy. An abortion. Case after case of women my age with my diagnosis—women who didn't survive or whose babies didn't make it.

I wanted to run, to disappear, but they told me I had to make a decision right then. They were liable. The pressure was unbearable.

I begged for another way. Finally, they told me they could cut the cancer out, but they warned me: *If we do this, your cancer will likely return, and you won't live past 40.*

It was a death sentence spoken over me: words that pierced through every hope, every dream, and every belief I had about my future. For years, I let those words shape my thoughts, emotions, and actions. I walked in fear. I carried discouragement. I battled hopelessness.

They applied a topical lidocaine, but it wasn't enough to dull the pain. With five people holding me down, I bit into a rubber ball as the doctor made each incision. Fifty stitches later, the wound was closed, but the battle was far from over.

As my pregnancy progressed, my growing belly pulled at the

scar, stretching it until it became an angry red mark—jagged and swollen, like a shark had torn through my side. I was devastated. Embarrassed. I struggled to accept what I saw in the mirror, unable to reconcile the image with the person I once was.

I felt stolen from. My confidence was at an all-time low. I felt that my future was destroyed and my impact was over. The first two years were a blur. I didn't talk about how I was doing on the inside. On the outside, I looked fine and told people I was fine.

But at home, in the quiet moments, I was drowning in fear. I spent endless hours researching every worst-case scenario. I was consumed with the "what ifs"—what if they were right? What if I didn't live past 40? What if my impact was truly over?

At 47 years old, the one thing I wish I could tell my 26-year-old self is that nobody and nothing can take it away from you. I have been cancer-free since I was 36 years old, and cancer is not my story anymore.

I didn't know it then, but the fight to hold onto my faith in that season became the foundation for how I now live, lead, and empower others.

LIVING OUT LOUD

I didn't always live this boldly. In fact, for a long time, I was too busy trying to fit into the mold I thought I was supposed to fill.

I graduated with a business administration degree, landed a sales job right out of college, and set my sights on the corporate ladder. I sold everything from software to uniforms! Yes, uniforms! Can you believe it? The funniest part of that job was that I had to wear a uniform that looked like a gas station attendant. Oh, if my former employer could only see me in the hot pink business suits I wear now! It wasn't glamorous, but it felt like the "right" thing to do.

I became an exceptionally successful Executive Recruiter for high-level tech jobs. Even though I didn't know anything about IT jobs, I have always been good at building relationships. Still, no matter how many promotions I earned, something felt off. I put on the pantyhose and the navy suit and tried to look the part. When you don't feel confident in your purpose, you do what you think other people want you to do.

I spent years searching for validation in the opinions of others. Deep down, I believed I wasn't worthy enough to step into *more*.

Today, I'm living proof of what happens when you let God activate your impact. And let me tell you, it doesn't always make sense to other people. I had just earned the honor of being named the youngest and fastest to reach "Global Distributor of the Year" for a network marketing company when I decided to make a bold move.

I left it all. That's right. I walked away from leading an annual sales volume of $3.9 million and a team of 80,000 distributors because I knew God was calling me to something different, something that would eventually change the course of my family's story.

Do you know what happened when I left? When I ventured outside of my comfort zone? When I listened to the whisper in my heart? It was better than I imagined and nothing that I feared. In just six months, I replaced a team and income that had taken me six years to build.

Along the way, I've appeared as an expert on NBC and CBS and been featured in *Forbes*, *Huffington Post*, and *InStyle Magazine*.

I've built multiple successful businesses and helped other women scale their purpose-driven brands. Today, my *Live Out Loud* memberships and masterminds draw women from all over the world.

Since 2017, every live event I've held at luxury hotels has sold out. My husband (also known as my BFF), whom I'm proud to say I've been married to for over 20 years, now works alongside me, and we have two beautiful, brilliant, and kind daughters.

But none of that qualifies me more than the battles I've fought and the breakthroughs I've experienced. I know what it's like to feel small, stuck, and silenced. And I know how to break free. I've been a witness, a guide, and a shoulder to cry on for the women who have found their own breakthroughs in my community.

Through *Live Out Loud*, I've created faith-first, nonjudgmental spaces where women can grow in confidence, clarity, and community—at every stage of their business journey. These are safe spaces rooted in bold belief, Kingdom purpose, and radical obedience to what God is calling each woman to do.

Ignite is our starter community, designed for women ready to go all in—personally, professionally, and spiritually. It's where faith gets activated, business foundations are built, and momentum starts to grow.

The *Live Out Loud Elite Mastermind* is for high-achieving women who are already building successful businesses but want to scale to seven figures *God's way*—with strategy, alignment, and strong faith at the center.

The Queen's Table is my most intimate and powerful space—a private mastermind for faith-driven founders and CEOs leading seven to 10-figure companies. These women are expanding their Kingdom impact with boldness, grace, and a deep sense of divine calling. It's a table for legacy-minded leaders who want to lead with excellence and be poured into at the highest level.

But breakthrough isn't about how much you make. It is available to anyone whose heart is open to it. I've seen it happen for women in a room of 75 and around an intimate table of 12. Because when women come together with hearts open to God's power, transformation is inevitable.

ACTIVATE YOUR IMPACT

That's why I'm uniquely equipped to help YOU step into your God-given impact—boldly, unapologetically, and fully alive.

Not because I'm extraordinary—but because I finally let God's extraordinary purpose move through me. And you can too.

THE POWER OF WHAT YOU SPEAK

We all have a choice. We can either partner with death or life, with darkness or light. I've learned that God's plan is always life, and we are meant to live in the light. That's how we step into impact. That's why I wrote this book—because your life matters. You were made for impact.

What you consume matters. It shapes what you believe. And what you believe shapes what you speak. And what you speak? That becomes what you live.

Success Requires Action

The activations in this book will help you break free from the thoughts, patterns, and beliefs that have kept you stuck and recognize the power in what you declare over your life. When you start speaking God's truth, you will see shifts. You will gain clarity, confidence, and boldness. You will begin to step into the impact you were created to make.

This isn't just about inspiration—it's about transformation. This book is designed to help you step into activation. Here's how to use it.

- **Pray & Be Open to Receive**—Ask God to reveal His truth to you.
- **Consume**—Take in a new, true story that aligns with God's promises.
- **Believe**—Let the truth take root in your heart.
- **Speak**—Declare God's promises over your life.
- **Take Action**—Walk boldly in the calling God has placed on your life.

A PRAYER TO BEGIN THIS JOURNEY

I believe in the power of prayer, and I want you to speak this prayer out loud over the experience you're about to have with this book. Expect the Holy Spirit to move in you, speak to you, and activate what has been inside you all along.

Heavenly Father,
I come before You with an open heart, ready to receive all that You have for me. I surrender my fears, doubts, and limitations at Your feet. Lord, I ask You to open my eyes to see clearly, open my ears to hear Your voice, and open my heart to fully embrace the purpose You have placed within me.

Holy Spirit, move in me. Activate the gifts inside of me. Show me where I am meant to make an impact in my business, my life, and my faith. Remove every obstacle standing in the way of my calling. Break every lie that has told me I am not enough. Replace my fear with bold faith, my doubt with confidence, and my hesitation with obedience.

ACTIVATE YOUR IMPACT

I believe that Jesus' blood covers me, that I am chosen, equipped, and created for such a time as this. I declare that I will no longer live in the shadows of fear or uncertainty. I will step into the fullness of who You have called me to be.

Lord, let this journey be one of transformation. Let Your Word come alive in my spirit. Let me be activated in a way that glorifies You and impacts those around me.

In Jesus' mighty name, I pray,
Amen

Your story is not over. God is ready to move, speak, and awaken something inside you that has been waiting to come alive.

Let's get started!

Before you dive in, text Prayer to (310) 564-7438 to listen to a short prayer from Brooke—inviting God to speak, lead, and activate your impact through every page of this book.

SECTION 1: BUSINESS

Chapter One

ACTIVATE YOUR PURPOSE

*"The thief comes only to steal and kill and destroy;
I have come that they may have life, and have it to the full"*
(John 10:10 NIV)

TWO VERSIONS OF YOU EXIST—
WHICH ONE WILL YOU BE?

There are two versions of you.

One version stays in hesitation—always waiting, questioning, and second-guessing if she's really meant for something greater. She lets fear dictate her decisions. She feels a tug in her spirit but silences it with excuses. She lets the opinions of others shape what she believes is possible. And before she knows it, years pass—her dreams still on the shelf, her calling untouched.

The other version? She is bold. She steps into divine confidence, fully knowing God has assigned her to something bigger than herself. She doesn't wait for perfect conditions—she moves in faith, even when she's afraid. She isn't concerned with the voices telling her it's impossible—she listens only to the voice of God.

Right now, you are choosing between these two versions of yourself. Whether you realize it or not, your next move determines which version of you will show up in this life.

So let me ask you—which one are you going to be?

I had a choice: let the fear of death shrink me or let the promise of God stretch me. I chose to stretch.

THE COST OF INACTION

Too many women hold back from stepping into the fullness of who they were created to be. They hesitate, wrestling with doubt. They let fear influence their decisions. Before they know it, time has passed—dreams still waiting, callings still unfulfilled.

Maybe you've felt this. The tug-of-war between who you are now and who you could be. Maybe you've even convinced yourself that you'll step into purpose "one day"—when you feel ready, when the fear is gone, when life is less complicated.

But let me tell you the truth: purpose doesn't wait.

The longer you delay, the longer you live beneath your calling. And let's be clear—the cost of inaction isn't just about you. There are people on the other side of your obedience—people who need what God has placed inside of you. If you don't activate your purpose, who misses out?

THE TRUTH ABOUT PURPOSE

Most people think purpose is something they find. They chase it like it's hidden, waiting to be discovered at the end of a perfect plan.

But that's a lie.

Purpose isn't found—it's activated.

ACTIVATE YOUR IMPACT

God has already placed it inside of you. He has been waiting for you to stop questioning, stop delaying, and start walking in it. Ephesians 2:10 tells you that you are God's masterpiece, and He created you so you can do the good things He planned for you.

Your purpose was set in motion before you were even born. The problem isn't that you don't have purpose—it's that you haven't fully stepped into it yet. You were made for a purpose. You are meant to fulfill your purpose on this earth.

IT'S TIME FOR A SHIFT

That pull you feel toward something greater? That's not your imagination.

I had that same feeling when my transformation began. It was in those dark days of doubt following my cancer diagnosis. It wasn't overnight, but deep inside, I started to feel a pull toward something greater. I began to think about my daughter —what legacy would I leave for her? I wanted her to know who I was and to see me living with purpose.

That desire led me to search for something more, and in that search, I discovered John 10:10. The truth is, I didn't like this scripture at first! John 10:10 says, *"The thief comes only to steal and kill and destroy; I have come that they may have life, and have it to the full"* (NIV).

The thief had certainly been stealing from me—stealing my confidence, my future, my ability to dream. But it was the second half of that scripture that changed everything for me. For the first time, I saw it differently. *Jesus came so that I could have life —abundant, overflowing, victorious life.* I started to speak to God at a different level, and for the first time, I heard Him like never before.

I carried with me a new sense of purpose. It fueled my drive to help others experience the same freedom. It's what led me to speak on stages around the country, share my story in magazines, and ultimately build businesses that empower women to create their own legacy of impact.

So often, we don't see or hear clearly, especially when we are in the middle of a storm. I want to give you the revelation faster than I found it because I was blind to it. I couldn't see it until the Holy Spirit revealed it.

Then, everything changed. I became awake, alert, and aware that a real thief is trying to rob us of our destiny. *But God!* But God calls us to live in overflow. But God calls us to live in abundance.

The thief comes to steal our future, kill our dreams, and destroy our confidence. But Jesus came to give us life. That scripture became my anchor. I had to decide if I would let the death sentence spoken over me define my life, or if I would choose to believe in God's promise of *life and overflow.*

Understanding the second part of John 10:10 is when my shift, my turning point, began. I had spent too long believing the words spoken over me, allowing fear to dictate my future. But Jesus came to bring life. He came to bring overflow. When I finally grasped that, I knew I had a choice: I could either stay stuck in the fear and limitations placed on me, or I could step into the truth of what God says about me.

I want that for you, too.

WHAT'S HOLDING YOU BACK?

I don't believe you're reading this book by accident. God has been preparing you for this moment—right now.

Every woman I have ever coached had a moment like this: a crossroads between staying comfortable or stepping into their calling.

ACTIVATE YOUR IMPACT

Some of them said yes. And their lives were transformed. Some of them hesitated. And years later, they're still stuck, wondering what could have been.

You are standing at the edge of a decision. Will you activate what God has placed inside of you?

TO ACTIVATE YOUR PURPOSE...

A few key shifts happen when you begin activating your purpose. Your perspective changes—you stop focusing on personal gain and start thinking about impact.

Even in uncertainty, you feel anchored in your calling with a deep conviction and peace. Doors start opening, and things align in ways you couldn't have orchestrated yourself. Fear may still be present, but it no longer holds you back—obedience takes the lead.

Suddenly, there's an urgency inside of you, a knowing that you must move forward. Activation is not about waiting; it's about stepping into what has already been set in motion for you.

TRESA'S STORY

WHEN PURPOSE FINDS YOU IN THE PROMISED LAND

Purpose isn't something you *find*—it's something you step into. And sometimes, stepping into purpose requires leaving everything you know behind.

That's exactly what happened to Tresa in 2017.

After spending 25 years in the medical field, she was comfortable. She had a stable career, a home she loved, and a life that made sense. But while working her 9-to-5, she was also teaching a Bible study—diving deep into the book of Joshua.

One verse kept stirring something inside her: *"Have I not*

commanded you? Be strong and courageous. Do not be afraid; do not be discouraged, for the Lord your God will be with you wherever you go" (Joshua 1:9, NIV).

Week after week, she taught it. And week after week, she felt God whispering, "Tresa, this is for you."

She decided that from that moment on, whenever she had a decision to make, she would always choose the bravest option—no hesitation, no overthinking.

Then came the moment of truth. Her sons, who had been having success as real estate investors, called her and said, "Mom, it's time. Quit your job, move to Dallas, and do this with us."

It was terrifying. It meant walking away from everything she had built—her career, her home, her friends, her ministry.

But she had already made the decision.

She was going to choose the brave thing.

She quit her job, sold her home, and moved to Dallas—stepping into real estate with nothing but faith and a willingness to learn. As she started buying properties—literally taking land—she couldn't help but think of Joshua leading the Israelites into the Promised Land.

But then something unexpected happened. She looked around and thought, *Where are all the women?*

There were men dominating the industry, but women like her—teachers, nurses, women making $65K to $100K a year—weren't stepping into this opportunity.

That's when she realized this wasn't just about real estate. *This was about purpose.* She wasn't just called to take land—she was called to help other women do the same.

So, with just 14 months of experience, she took another bold leap: launching The Women's Real Estate Investors Network.

The first meeting? Forty women showed up.

Then COVID hit.

Her in-person events shut down, and she had to pivot

overnight. With zero experience in online business, she started a virtual masterclass, and 699 women showed up.

The next month? 1,200. By the end of the year, her network had grown substantially. Since 2019, her network has served over 250,000 women.

And now? Tresa runs the largest women's real estate investment network in the country.

But purpose doesn't stop at success. There was still more.

Amidst all the business growth, Tresa found she needed a space where she could be poured into, where she could surround herself with faith-filled women who understood the weight of leadership.

That's when I called her. I knew she needed the *Queen's Table*. And when I invited her in, she said yes.

She found business partners, lifelong friendships, and a faith-centered sisterhood that lifted her up, poured wisdom into her, and stood with her through every challenge.

Now, she's stepping into an even *greater* assignment—Fellowship on Fire, a faith-based community of women growing in God together.

Because *this* is what purpose does. It builds. It expands. It leads you to something bigger than you could have ever imagined.

So let me ask you: Where is God calling you to step into purpose?

What is that thing you keep putting off because it feels too big, too unknown, or too risky?

Remember: *Purpose isn't something you wait for.* It's something you step into.

It's time.

WHAT DOES IT MEAN TO ACTIVATE YOUR PURPOSE?

You were born on purpose, for a purpose. No matter what season you're in or what setbacks you've faced, your life has a God-ordained assignment. But let me ask you—are you living with bold clarity on that purpose? Or are you hesitating, questioning, and shrinking back because of fear, doubt, or the voices of others?

The word purpose is often misunderstood. The dictionary defines purpose as "the reason for which something is done or created or for which something exists."

I went down a biblical path to make sure I could discover my purpose and ensure it was unshakable. I discovered that we were born on purpose and for a purpose. God has created us to fulfill that purpose on this earth. That's why purpose is the foundation. If we're going to activate the impact we're meant to make, we must first know and understand our God-given purpose.

Biblical purpose goes deeper—it is about God's divine intention for your life. It is not based on what you do but on who you are.

For years, I let fear dictate my life. I allowed words spoken over me to become a death sentence to my dreams.

But God never designed us to live under the weight of someone else's expectations or limitations. He designed us to step fully into our purpose, to live with confidence in His plan, and to declare His promises over our lives. Purpose isn't just something we discover—it's something we ACTIVATE. Today, I want to show you how.

WHAT DRIVES ME?

One of the most powerful transformations I witness in my work is when a woman activates her purpose. I have seen women go from doubting themselves, feeling stuck, and questioning their worth to stepping into their God-given callings with boldness and clarity.

This is why I do what I do.

I remember the moment I realized my own calling—to activate the gifts inside other women and help them fully step into their purpose. It wasn't a lightning bolt moment but rather a series of encounters with women who had everything they needed but were waiting for someone to call it out in them.

That's when I knew—*this* is my work. This is why I show up every day. This book is an extension of that calling. It's a tool to help you step into the bold life God has for you.

PURPOSE AS THE ULTIMATE TRANSFORMATION

When a woman activates her purpose, everything shifts. Mindset, confidence, relationships, and even business success—it all changes. Why? Because purpose isn't about striving; it's about stepping into alignment with who God created you to be.

The greatest transformation I have ever witnessed is not external success—it's a woman realizing, "I was made for this." That moment of revelation is life-changing, and it's the reason I keep going.

This book isn't just for reading—it's for activating. It's for taking action. It's for bold moves. By the end of this chapter, I want you to take the first step toward activating your purpose.

You've been waiting long enough. Purpose isn't passive—it's a decision. The journey through this book will unlock and activate your next level.

Your purpose is waiting. It's time to activate it.

ACTIVATION 1: IGNITE YOUR PASSION

"God will continually revitalize you, implanting within you the passion to do what pleases him."
(Philippians 2:13, TPT)

Passion fuels purpose! The two are connected. Passion drives purpose forward and makes it come alive inside of you. Without passion, purpose feels distant—like something you know exists but aren't fully living out.

When passion is ignited, purpose is activated.

Passion is defined as "a strong and barely containable emotion." I LOVE being around passionate people because their energy is contagious! They have big dreams and chase bold visions. Their purpose usually drives them, and they believe they will make the world a better place. They are fully awake and activated to do what they are called to do!

So, let me ask you—how passionate are you right now about your life and what you are being called to? There have been seasons where I felt like my passion had dimmed, where I wanted to reignite it but didn't know how. We all have those moments. But here's what I want you to know: you can reignite your passion in an instant!

Our scripture today says that God implants passion inside of us! That means passion isn't something you *lose*—it sometimes gets buried. And what God gives, no one can take away. If you feel your passion has been buried under doubt, discouragement, or exhaustion, it's time to uncover it. It's already inside of you!

Let's go even deeper—do you know why it's called *The Passion of the Christ*? The word "passion" comes from the Latin *passio*, meaning to suffer. Jesus' passion was His willingness to endure suffering for a greater purpose—our redemption. His passion was sacrificial, powerful, and unstoppable.

ACTIVATE YOUR IMPACT

Now, think about your life. What have you suffered? What experiences have shaped you? What moments felt like obstacles but were actually preparing you for something greater?

That is where passion is stirred up! That passion—born out of your struggles, your battles, and even your pain—fuels you forward into purpose.

Maybe the very thing that feels silent in your life has never been fully acknowledged. Perhaps you've been working, striving, and pushing forward without true passion. It's time to awaken it. Passion isn't just about excitement—it's about conviction. It's about stepping into what God created you to do, even when it's hard.

Oftentimes, you are called to do the very thing you fear the most. If you're called to speak, you may feel attacked in your voice. If you're called to lead, you may battle doubt and insecurity. The enemy always tries to silence you in the area where you are meant to shine the brightest. But not today.

It might feel like your passion is under a blanket right now, but I know deep down, there's still a fire inside of you. I want you to connect with it and let God breathe life into it. Ask Him to revitalize your passion, make your heart beat with excitement again, and accelerate your progress with inspired ideas and strategies.

It's time for a Holy Spirit encounter that reignites your soul. And it starts by speaking it out loud.

SPEAK THIS OUT LOUD:

God, I declare that You have given me a passion that cannot be stolen! I am excited to chase what pleases You. My passion is reignited, and I am alive with purpose!

ACTIVATION 2: YOU WERE BORN FOR THIS MOMENT

"Who knows if perhaps you were made queen for just such a time as this?"
(Esther 4:14, NLT)

You are not here by accident. Everything about your life—your gifts, your experiences, even your challenges—has positioned you for this moment.

You are not reading this by accident. Right now, in this very moment, you are being called into activation. Your purpose is not in the future—it's in the now. God has placed you in this exact time, in this exact season, for a reason.

Esther's story is a powerful example of stepping into divine timing. She went from an unknown woman to a queen in the blink of an eye. But what made her truly great?

- Her courage
- Her willingness to choose faith over fear
- Her unwavering conviction that God had placed her there for a reason

When her people were in danger, she had a choice. She could shrink back and stay silent or rise up and activate her purpose. Esther risked everything because she believed God had prepared her for that exact moment.

Because she said YES, she saved a nation.

I had my own Esther moment when I became a mother and felt the pressure of choosing between being a present mom and pursuing my God-given calling in business. People told me I had to pick one—I couldn't have both. But God had already spoken to me: Start the business.

For years, I wrestled with doubt. What if I failed at both?

What if I wasn't enough? But I chose to trust God and do it differently. I didn't have a roadmap—I just remained obedient. I ignored the voices that told me it was impossible.

Now, 20 years later, my daughters thank me for taking that leap of faith. They watched me build, they saw me trust, and they are walking in their own purpose because of it.

The first 5–10 years were hard. I wondered if I was making the right choice. But I kept going. Now I stand on the other side, saying thank God I did it.

Now, it's your turn. What decision, opportunity, or calling is right in front of you that requires faith? What is your Esther moment?

It will take courage. It will require activated faith. It will mean choosing to act even when you are afraid. But you can. You were born for this.

SPEAK THIS OUT LOUD:

God, I declare that I was born for such a time as this! I reject fear and step boldly into my calling. My situation, surroundings, and setbacks do not define what's possible—You do!

ACTIVATION 3: YOUR TRIAL, YOUR TRAINING

"Count it all joy, my brothers, when you meet trials of various kinds, for you know that the testing of your faith produces steadfastness. And let steadfastness have its full effect, that you may be perfect and complete, lacking in nothing."
(James 1:2-4, ESV)

THE WEIGHT OF RESISTANCE IS THE STRENGTH OF YOUR CALLING

Every great calling comes with resistance. It's easy to think that opposition means you're off track. That setbacks signal failure. That obstacles mean God has forgotten you. But what if resistance isn't a sign to stop but rather a confirmation that you're stepping into something greater?

Look at the life of Jesus—His path to resurrection went through suffering. David wasn't crowned king without first facing Goliath. Joseph's dream wasn't fulfilled until he endured betrayal, slavery, and imprisonment. The weight of resistance wasn't the enemy of their calling—the refining process prepared them to carry it.

What if your biggest frustration, which feels like a constant battle, is actually shaping you into the leader, the visionary, the world-changer God created you to be?

GOD IS NOT WASTING YOUR TRIAL

James 1:2-4 calls us to an unnatural response—joy in the midst of struggle. Why? Because trials are not meaningless. They have a purpose. They develop something in you that comfort never could:

- Endurance. True perseverance is not built in ease, but in pressing forward when everything in you wants to quit.
- Faith that withstands. A faith untested is a faith unproven. When you've walked through the fire and seen God sustain you, your trust in Him becomes unshakable.
- Preparation for the next level. The weight you carry

now is conditioning you for the greater responsibility, the greater impact, and the greater influence ahead.

THE RED SEA PRINCIPLE: WHAT SEEMS LIKE A DEAD END IS ACTUALLY A WAY THROUGH

When the Israelites were standing at the edge of the Red Sea, it looked like their story was over. Pharaoh's army was closing in, and there was no visible way forward. But what seemed like an impossible obstacle was actually the setup for the greatest deliverance they had ever seen.

The same is true for you. The trial you're facing is not the end of your story. It's the moment God is setting the stage for a breakthrough. What feels like a closed door may be the very thing that leads to your greatest opportunity.

God does His most miraculous work in the moments when human solutions run out.

YOUR OBSTACLE IS YOUR REFINING FIRE

Gold is purified in fire. Diamonds are formed under pressure. Swords are forged in heat. Strength is built through resistance.

Your challenge is not sent to destroy you. It is sent to refine you. To strip away the doubt, insecurity, fear, and comfort that keep you from walking fully in the power and authority God has given you.

Do not despise the process. Embrace it. Every hardship, every "no," every delay, every betrayal—is a tool in God's hands to shape you into the warrior He has called you to be.

SPEAK THIS OUT LOUD:

God, I trust You in my trials. I refuse to see obstacles as roadblocks, but instead as refining moments that are shaping me for greater things. I choose joy—not because it's easy, but because I know You are working in me, strengthening me, and preparing me. I will not be defeated. I will not shrink back. I will stand firm, knowing that what the enemy meant for evil, You will use for good. My obstacle is my preparation. My resistance is my refinement. And my breakthrough is on the way!

DECLARE YOUR PURPOSE IS ACTIVATED

I DECLARE I was born on purpose, for a purpose. God has called me, and I will not shrink back—I step boldly into my assignment!

I DECLARE my passion is reignited. What God has placed inside of me cannot be stolen. I move with energy, excitement, and conviction!

I DECLARE fear and doubt have no hold on me. I refuse to let the opinions of others or past setbacks define me—I walk in confidence and clarity!

I DECLARE this is my time to activate my purpose. I am not waiting for the perfect moment—I am stepping into God's plan now!

I DECLARE that what God starts, He will complete. Every obstacle is a setup for greater impact. I trust His process and move forward in faith!

ACTIVATE YOUR IMPACT

LOL ACTIVATION

You were made for impact—but have you fully activated it? So many people are walking around asleep to what they are called to do, allowing fear, doubt, and distractions to keep them from stepping into the life God has already prepared for them. Not you. Not anymore.

You've just consumed the truth that ignites your purpose. Now, it's time to go deeper. What you consume is what you believe. What you believe is what you speak. And what you speak is what you live out. This is where activation happens—when you stop hesitating and start walking in confidence, knowing God has already qualified and called you.

Let's do this. With an open heart, bold faith, and a commitment to action, answer the following questions:

LEARN IT:

What has been holding you back from fully activating your purpose? What fears, doubts, or outside voices have you allowed to slow you down?

OWN IT:

What step have you been avoiding that you know God is calling you to take? Where have you been hesitating instead of trusting Him completely?

LIVE IT:

If you chose to activate your purpose today—without fear, without hesitation—what would change? What would it look like to walk in full obedience and bold faith? Now, write down one action step you will take right now to move forward!

Chapter Two

ACTIVATE YOUR CREATIVITY

I used to believe I wasn't creative.

Maybe you've thought the same thing.

For years, I assumed creativity was reserved for artists, musicians, and designers—people with talents I didn't have. I couldn't draw. I wasn't a natural singer. So, I labeled myself as *not creative* and moved on.

But then I discovered the truth: We are all creative beings because we are **created in the image of God.**

> *"So God created mankind in His own image, in the image of God He created them; male and female He created them."*
> **(Genesis 1:27, NIV)**

God is the Creator. The One who spoke the entire universe into existence. And if we are made in His image, then that means creativity isn't a gift given to a select few—it's part of our very design.

> *Creativity isn't limited to artistic ability. It's in the way we think, the way we build, the way we lead, and the way we bring ideas to life.*

It's how a mother raises her children.
It's how an entrepreneur builds a business.
It's how a teacher inspires a student.
It's how a leader casts vision.
It's how we use our gifts to impact the world.

Creativity is problem-solving, storytelling, designing, speaking, and innovating. It's taking what's in your heart and making it real.

For so long, I believed I wasn't creative—until I stopped labeling myself and started seeing the unique ways God had wired me to create.

Everything you need is already inside you. It's time to activate it.

CREATIVITY UNLOCKS POSSIBILITIES

I didn't always know I was made for more. But deep down, I felt it.

I knew I was meant to create something meaningful, but I didn't know what or how. I had gone to college, earned a business degree, and stepped into entrepreneurship, but the world kept telling me I had to choose.

You can either be a mother or a businesswoman—not both.

ACTIVATE YOUR IMPACT

I rejected that.

I got my real estate license. I built businesses. I pursued what I was passionate about. But I still felt like something was missing—there were gaps in my skill set that I wasn't sure how to fill.

One of those gaps was in my own kitchen. I remember looking at my daughters one day and realizing *I had no idea how to cook.*

At that point, I had become certified in nutrition and understood that what we put in our bodies matters for long-term health. But when it came to actually preparing meals? I felt paralyzed.

I wanted to feed my family well. I wanted my daughters to grow up knowing how to nourish their bodies and make healthy choices. But I didn't know where to start.

So, I did what I knew to do: I started learning.

I bought cookbooks and immediately felt overwhelmed. They were filled with complex recipes and foreign techniques I didn't understand. I kept thinking, *I never want my daughters to feel this way.*

So, instead of giving up, I experimented.

I took overwhelming 20+ ingredient recipes and simplified them. I played with flavors and tested what worked. I made a mess in the kitchen. It wasn't always pretty, but something started to shift.

I wasn't just learning how to cook—I was activating my creativity.

I turned my simplified recipes into a cookbook called *The Thankful 30* because I was *so thankful* to have 30 recipes that actually tasted delicious. Then, I created a crockpot edition filled with simple, healthy meals.

Looking back at that title, I remember being so hard on myself for not coming up with something "more creative."

I thought, *Am I even creative enough to name my own book?*

If I could go back and tell young Brooke anything, I would tell her: *"You are more creative than you realize."*

The words we speak over ourselves matter. The thoughts we entertain shape our reality. I spent too much time listening to the wrong voices—the ones telling me I shouldn't, couldn't, or wouldn't.

But looking back now? I see how creative I really was. I never planned to become a cookbook author. But that's what happens when you activate your creativity—you unlock possibilities you never saw before.

It didn't stop there.

One day, a producer from NBC *Charlotte Today* reached out. She heard about my healthy protein bars and wanted me to share my recipes on their live show as a "Mom on a Mission."

I was terrified. I wasn't a professional chef. I didn't have a system. My kitchen was a mess half the time. But I said yes anyway. And let me tell you—I almost burned down the set my first time on TV! But they brought me back.

That one opportunity led to eight years of appearing on that show, sharing healthy recipes, nutrition tips, and even grocery shopping guides that helped families make better choices.

I went on to:

- Develop grocery shopping keychains before meal-planning apps existed.
- Teach families how to shop and pack healthy lunches.
- Speak at schools and hospitals about simple, healthy living.
- Sell my healthy lifestyle program to corporations—starting at $4,500 and eventually licensing the same exact program for $45,000+ per sale.

Looking back, I see how all of this started with one simple decision: I stopped believing I wasn't creative.

ACTIVATE YOUR IMPACT

I gave myself permission to learn, experiment, and build something new.

> Scan the QR code to download The Thankful 30 cookbooks—simple, healthy recipes that sparked a journey of creativity, confidence, and unexpected impact.

If you've ever believed that you're not creative, that your ideas don't matter, that what's inside of you isn't enough, it's time to break that mindset. You were created to create.

Everything about you—your gifts, your passions, your story—was intentionally placed inside of you by God. He didn't make a mistake.

For me, I spent decades allowing discouragement, disappointment, and doubt to delay my creativity. But the moment I shifted my perspective, everything changed.

So let's shift yours today. Let's activate the creativity that's been inside you all along.

ACTIVATION 1: UNLOCK YOUR CREATIVE POWER

"For we are God's handiwork, created in Christ Jesus to do good works, which God prepared in advance for us to do."
(Ephesians 2:10, NIV)

Let this Truth soak into your spirit right now:

- God chose you for this moment in time.
- You are God's idea!
- You are God's dream wrapped in flesh.
- You are a divine design, but more than anything, you are a divine desire (a true one of a kind)!
- You are wanted!
- You MATTER.
- You are loved.
- You are a masterpiece.

You are uniquely created. You are one-of-a-kind (and that's a good thing). He calls you His masterpiece.

The Creator of the Universe took great care in how He designed you. How incredible! And now He wants to AWAKEN the gifts, talents, and desires that He deposited in you—so you can walk out your calling. And your calling in life has God-given creative power to back it up!

Here's what I know: One of the main ways that successful, high-performing, creative women get taken out is by discouragement. For me, I spent decades speaking out the subtle lie: *"I'm not creative ..."*

But even when we don't feel creative, the truth remains—we are creative. God designed each of us with a unique ability that He loves to watch us use for His glory. Singing, dancing, writing code, designing buildings, leading cities, running companies—there's no limit to the ways He allows creativity to flow through us. That's how we show off the creativity God placed inside of us!

Whatever your unique talent is, it's a creative expression of how God wants to bless you and the people around you.

ACTIVATE YOUR IMPACT

ACTIVATION 2: STIR UP YOUR CREATIVE GIFTS

"We have different gifts, according to the grace given to each of us. If your gift is prophesying, then prophesy in accordance with your faith."
(Romans 12:6, NIV)

God has already placed gifts inside of you. Not just any gifts—gifts with divine intention. That means you don't have to force creativity. You don't have to strive. You don't have to compare.

Creativity is a supernatural flow that God built into you before you even knew it existed! When you align with Him, your creativity becomes a powerful tool for Kingdom impact.

Here's what I know: One of the biggest lies the enemy tells creative women is: "You're not good enough." Not creative enough. Not talented enough. Not unique enough.

But let me remind you: Your creativity is not about *you*. It's about what GOD wants to do through you.

I used to believe that creativity only belonged to artists. That unless I could paint a masterpiece, write a novel, or design something stunning, I wasn't *really* creative.

But creativity isn't limited to traditional art. God has deposited gifts in you that show up in ways you may not even realize:

- The way you solve problems in your business.
- The way you bring people together and build relationships.
- The way you dream up new ideas and boldly take action.

Creativity is in your DNA. And when you allow yourself to operate in the creative gifts God has given you, you step into your *divine assignment*—where His power meets your obedience.

Right now, let's activate that gift inside of you.

Take a moment to ask God:

- *What creative gifts have You placed in me that I've overlooked?*
- *Where have I let fear or comparison hold me back from using my gifts?*
- *How do You want to use my creativity for impact?*

Write down what He reveals to you.

Now, move forward in boldness because your creativity is meant to *build, bless, and impact*!

ACTIVATE YOUR IMPACT

SPEAK THIS OUT LOUD:

God, I trust You as my Creator. I refuse to believe the lie that I am not creative. I declare that I am made in Your image—designed to build, innovate, and bring ideas to life. I will not limit myself. I will not shrink back. I will step into my creative potential with boldness, knowing that You have already equipped me. My creativity is not lacking—it is waiting to be activated. I release fear, doubt, and hesitation, and I embrace the gifts You have placed inside of me. My creativity is unlocked, and I will use it for Your glory!

DECLARE YOUR CREATIVITY IS ACTIVATED

I DECLARE I am created to create! God designed me with purpose, and I will boldly use my creativity to impact the world.
I DECLARE my creative gifts are ignited! What God has placed inside of me cannot be hidden. I move with clarity, confidence, and vision.
I DECLARE fear and doubt have no hold on me! I refuse to let past failures or insecurities define me—I walk in bold creativity and endless possibilities.
I DECLARE this is my time to activate my creativity! I will not wait for permission. I will step forward and create now.
I DECLARE that what God starts, He will complete! My creativity is not wasted. Every idea, project, and gift is being used for a greater purpose.

LOL ACTIVATION

You were created to create—but have you fully activated it? So many people walk around believing they are not creative, allowing doubt, fear, and distractions to keep them from bringing their ideas to life. Not you. Not anymore.

You've just consumed truth that ignites your creative power. Now, it's time to go deeper. This is where activation happens—when you stop hesitating and start creating with confidence, knowing God has already given you everything you need.

So let's do this. With an open heart, bold faith, and a commitment to action, answer the following questions:

LEARN IT:

What limiting beliefs have you held about your creativity? Where have you doubted your ability to create?

OWN IT:

What creative step have you been avoiding? What project, idea, or vision have you delayed because of fear or doubt?

LIVE IT:

If you fully activated your creativity today—without fear or hesitation—what would change? What is one action step you will take right now to move forward?

Chapter Three

ACTIVATE YOUR CONFIDENCE

Confidence isn't something you're born with; it's something you activate. It's built through experiences, struggles, and faith—through choosing to believe what God says about you instead of what the world has labeled you.

For most of my life, I didn't feel confident. In fact, I believed confidence was something people were either born with or not, and I wasn't one of the lucky ones.

As a child, I was insecure. I was made fun of for my fair, freckly skin. I never understood why people teased others, because when I looked at someone, I saw their heart. I saw their beauty. I never wanted to tear anyone down because I knew exactly how words could hurt. I became someone who used kindness and humor as protection—if I could make people laugh, if I could love them well, maybe they wouldn't criticize me.

That insecurity stayed with me. And then came the label.

Growing up, I loved to talk. I had so much energy and excitement—I always had something to say! But then, one day, I was given a name: *Babbling Brooke.*

I'll never forget the moment it happened. I was in a room, bursting with excitement to share something, and someone said, "Oh, don't pay attention to her. She's just babbling. Babbling Brooke." At first, I laughed along, but deep inside, it stung. That label followed me. Adults started using it, too—not out of malice, but they didn't realize how it would shape me.

Slowly, I started to shrink back. I second-guessed my words. I wondered if I was talking too much. The enemy used that label to convince me that my voice didn't matter. That my energy was too much. That I should quiet down.

And I did. For years, I let that name hold me back. But in 2021, everything changed.

I was preparing for one of my *Live Out Loud* events, and I kept asking God what He wanted me to speak over the women coming into the room. I wanted them to feel joy, but I didn't know what was holding them back. So I dove into the book of Philippians—because if there's any book in the Bible that speaks about joy, it's Philippians.

And then, God gave me a revelation that wrecked me. I discovered that in Philippians, the word joy is defined in two ways: calm delight and extreme hilarity.

Extreme hilarity? That's me! The energy, the laughter, the passion—I finally saw that God made me this way on purpose! But then I read the phrase calm delight, and suddenly, insecurity crept in again. *I want to be calm delight … that seems more respectable. Maybe my energy is too much.*

In that moment, I prayed: *Lord, show me what calm delight really means.*

Then I Googled the phrase.

Author Joyce Meyer describes calm delight as "a bubbling brook that just flows along quietly and peacefully, bringing refreshment to everything and everyone along its path."

A bubbling brook.

I sat there and wept. The Lord completely replaced the label that had once held me back. I was never meant to be Babbling Brooke.

I was always a Bubbling Brooke—bringing refreshment, joy, and life to those around me. That's who I always was. And God made that clear to me in a single moment.

That's what I want for *you* today.

God never intended for you to live under labels that shrink you. The enemy has tried to attack your confidence because he knows how powerful your voice is when you step into who God has called you to be.

What labels have you carried that were never meant to define you?

What false names have tried to limit your confidence?

SHIRLEY'S STORY

FINDING YOUR VOICE, WALKING IN BOLDNESS, AND BEING SET FREE

God used one moment to set Shirley free.

There are moments in life when God's presence is so undeniable that unbelief no longer has a place in your life. Instead, belief in His calling becomes the driving force that propels you forward in faith.

It was February 2020, in a room full of powerful business women of faith at one of my *Live Out Loud* retreats.

Shirley was obedient and followed God's call to be in that room, but I could sense something holding her back.

Prayer was never a big part of Shirley's life growing up. She knew the prayers taught in school by heart but never experienced the kind of deep, intimate conversations with God that she witnessed happening in that room.

As she listened to these women pray with boldness, passion, and authority, her heart whispered, *I want to talk to God like that. I want to pray like that.*

Then, she spoke up, vulnerably. "I want to pray like that. I have Jeremiah 29:11 tattooed on my arm," she said. "For me, it's my way of talking to God and holding on to His promises."

In that moment, I felt the Holy Spirit nudge me to challenge her to pray out loud. I looked her in the eye and felt a heart-to-heart connection so strong that I felt prompted to ask, "What does that scripture really mean to you?" I asked her to say it out loud in front of everyone.

Silence.

I watched as it seemed like something was pressing down on her chest, trying to steal her voice. Fear. Doubt. The weight of unbelief. The enemy did not want her to declare God's promises over her life.

But I wasn't going to let that happen.

I laid hands on her and invited the room to pray with boldness, authority, and expectation with her. We all fought for her breakthrough, declaring that she was free from whatever was holding her back. And then, right there in that room, God set her free.

It was one moment, but it changed everything.

That day, the seed of her purpose was activated. She went from questioning her belief to walking in it boldly. She went from keeping her faith private to building a faith-based gym in Oregon—during a pandemic. She went from praying in silence to praying over her community—watching lives be transformed through the power of prayer.

She stopped worrying about offending people with her faith and started walking confidently with Jesus every single day.

She was activated.

ACTIVATE YOUR IMPACT

And now? God is using her to activate others. The best part about this story is that Shirley opened a door in my community that paved the way for hundreds of other women to be set free.

Recently, I hosted another retreat in the same room at the Ritz-Carlton, Laguna Niguel, with a different group of women. I shared Shirley's story, and it opened up the conversation to several women who felt the same way about praying out loud. They desired to be set free and confidentially and boldly pray and worship. Guess what? They left that room completely on fire and claimed victory over that same fear!

Shirley's story is proof that when we get in the right room, the right atmosphere of belief, and choose to fully step into belief, everything shifts. We stop questioning. We stop hesitating. We stop holding back. Instead, we move with boldness, power, and certainty in the plans God has for us.

And I want you to know that the same God who set Shirley free is calling you into that same freedom.

You are here on purpose for a purpose. It's time to believe it.

CONFIDENCE IS A CHOICE

The world teaches us that confidence comes from success, approval, or natural ability. But true, unshakable confidence is biblical—it is something we step into by faith.

> *"For the Spirit God gave us does not make us timid, but gives us power, love, and self-discipline."*
> **(2 Timothy 1:7, NIV)**

God has already given you everything you need to walk in confidence. It is not something you need to *find*—it is something you *activate*.

That activation starts with a choice.

I had to learn this firsthand. People assume I've always been confident, that speaking comes naturally to me, and that I've never been nervous in my life. But that's not true.

For years, whenever I was handed a microphone, my hands would shake, my face would turn red, and my voice would crack. I would feel the anxiety building inside me, knowing all eyes were on me. I wanted to get better, so I took responsibility for my growth.

I hired a speaking coach. I committed to scaling up. I practiced over and over again. But through this process, I realized something deeper—I was more of a people-pleaser than I thought. I was too focused on myself. I was worried about what others thought of me instead of focusing on why I was there and what I was called to do.

One day, something shifted. I had been praying for confidence and relief, asking God to take away the fear that gripped me every time I stepped on stage. And in that moment, He gave me a new vision—one that changed everything.

I realized I was only there to serve an audience of One. God had created me. He had called me. And in that moment, I envisioned Jesus standing at the back of the room, watching—not with judgment, but with love.

I wasn't speaking to impress a crowd. I wasn't there to prove anything. I was there to be obedient, to deliver the message I had been given, and to serve the people He had placed in front of me.

Then I asked myself: "Who is on the other side of my obedience?" Even if I impacted just one person, wouldn't it be worth it?

That's when the pressure lifted. The fear lost its power. It was never about me—it was about trusting that if God called me to speak, He would equip me for it.

That's the moment confidence began to rise. Not because I suddenly felt more capable, but because I finally understood that my job was simply to show up and let God do the rest.

ACTIVATE YOUR IMPACT

I realized I had been making it about *me* this entire time. My lack of confidence was never about my ability—it was about my focus.

When I turned my nervous stomach and anxiety into excitement, everything changed. Instead of worrying about what I would say wrong, I focused on who I was there to serve.

Confidence didn't come overnight. I was really bad. Then less bad. Then okay. Then decent. Then good. But one day, after years of showing up, the fear fell off. I finally felt like I was born to do this.

Now I know that confidence is not just for a select few—it is available to anyone who is willing to take responsibility for their growth and make a choice to trust God over fear. You don't have to wait years for confidence. You can have a moment where confidence is activated.

God never intended for you to carry labels that diminish you. Your confidence is under attack because your voice carries power when you fully embrace who God has called you to be.

What labels have you carried that were never meant to define you?

What false names have tried to limit your confidence?

Today, throw off those old labels, shift your focus, and step fully into the confidence God has already placed inside of you.

SHINE & BE SURROUNDED

I've seen women's entire lives change because they decided to step into the light and be fully who God called them to be. I've watched confidence come alive in them the moment they embraced their true identity, free from hesitation.

This is why stepping into a community of women who cheer you on is so powerful. We need people around us who don't let us shrink back—who say, "Yes! Let's go!" and launch us into action.

I believe we have a responsibility in our communities to speak life, to encourage, to be the ones saying, "You go, girl!" because that one word of encouragement might be the push she needs to step forward.

The truth is, we don't always know if things will work out for someone. But that's not our responsibility. Our responsibility is to cheer them on, to call out their greatness, and to remind them of who they were created to be. Because if they never step into the light and let their confidence shine, we'll never know what they were capable of.

Confidence creates. It allows us to build, innovate, and make an impact. That's the whole purpose of having confidence in the first place.

So today, make the choice. Step forward. Surround yourself with people who push you toward purpose. And be that encouragement for someone else.

Your confidence is waiting to be activated. Let's go.

ACTIVATION 1: LAY IT DOWN AND THROW IT OFF!

"Therefore, since we are surrounded by such a great cloud of witnesses, let us throw off everything that hinders and the sin that so easily entangles. And let us run with perseverance the race marked out for us."
(Hebrews 12:1, NIV)

Imagine trying to run a marathon while carrying a heavy backpack filled with rocks. Every step would feel harder and every movement slower. It would be exhausting, discouraging, and nearly impossible to reach the finish line.

This is exactly what happens when we carry the weight of things God never intended us to hold onto.

ACTIVATE YOUR IMPACT

- **Unforgiveness** clings to your heart, making it impossible to experience freedom.
- **Shame** whispers that you're not good enough, keeping you from stepping boldly into your calling.
- **Fear** holds you back, making you hesitate when you were meant to run.
- **Labels** spoken over you in childhood still echo in your mind, limiting how you see yourself today.

But here's the truth: God has already marked a race for you to run. He wants you to run with perseverance, free from the weight of past hurts, doubts, or insecurities. Anything that tries to hold you back, slow you down, or make you question your worth is not from Him.

But today, you're making a decision. It's time to throw off what hinders you.

Faith Activation

1. Take out a sheet of paper and write down everything that has been stopping, delaying, hindering, or binding you. The words. The wounds. The worries. The shame. The unforgiveness. The past mistakes. Lay it all down on paper.
2. Now, cross them out. Tear up the paper. Burn it if you have to. Physically throw it away. As you do, declare out loud: "I release everything that has weighed me down. I throw off every burden and step fully into the race God has marked for me."
3. Speak this truth over yourself: "I am running my race with perseverance. I lay down every weight, every label, every burden. I am free to move forward!"

God didn't call you to carry burdens—He called you to run. Let this be the moment where you step into the freedom that was always yours.

ACTIVATION 2: OVERFLOW WITH LOVE!

"How deeply intimate and far-reaching is His love! How enduring and inclusive it is! Endless love beyond measurement that transcends our understanding— this extravagant love pours into you until you are filled to overflowing with the fullness of God!"
(Ephesians 3:18-19, TPT)

Confidence isn't just about believing in yourself—it's about knowing how deeply you are loved by the One who created you. When you root your confidence in God's love, you stop striving for approval from others. You stop questioning your worth. You stop shrinking back in fear because you are anchored in something unshakable: His never-ending, extravagant love.

The enemy wants to convince you that love is something you must earn. That you are only worthy when you perform, when you achieve, when you get everything right. But God's love is not conditional or based on what you do—it is based on who He is.

When you allow His love to fill you, it overflows. You don't have to force confidence; it naturally rises up within you because you know you are secure in Him. From that place, you can pour love into others, becoming a reflection of God's heart to the world.

That's the kind of confidence God wants you to have. Not a surface-level confidence that crumbles under pressure but an unshakable confidence that stands strong no matter what storms come your way.

This kind of confidence is not built overnight. It is built through faith, perseverance, and trusting God's promises, even when you can't see the outcome yet. It is a confidence that says: *Even when I don't feel it, I know who I am. Even when I don't see the way, I know God is leading me.*

It's time to stop questioning your worth. Stop second-guessing if you have what it takes. You do because God has already placed everything you need inside of you. Now, it's time to walk in it.

Faith Activation

1. **Define Your Unshakable Confidence.** Write down what unshakable confidence means to you. Is it trusting God's plan fully? Is it standing firm even when fear tries to creep in? Be specific.
2. **Speak It Out Loud.** Every morning, declare this over yourself: *I stand firm in my identity in Christ. My confidence is unshakable. Nothing can move me from God's promises!*
3. **Take a Bold Step.** Confidence grows when you take action. Do something today that pushes you beyond fear into confidence—whether it's speaking, launching, writing, or stepping into a leadership moment.

SPEAK THIS OUT LOUD:

God, I trust You as my source of confidence. I refuse to believe the lie that I am not enough. I declare that I am made in Your image—bold, strong, and filled with purpose. I will not shrink back. I will not let fear, doubt, or the words of others define me. I choose to believe what You say about me. I throw off every label that was never meant to define me, and I step into the unshakable confidence that You have already placed inside of me. My confidence is not lacking—it is being activated. I release fear, hesitation, and insecurity, and I embrace the boldness You have called me to walk in. I will stand firm, shine bright, and overflow with the fullness of Your love. I am confident because You created me to be.

DECLARE YOUR CONFIDENCE IS ACTIVATED!

I DECLARE I am fearfully and wonderfully made. God has designed me with purpose, and I stand boldly in my identity.
I DECLARE my confidence is unshakable. No label, no lie, no past mistake can hold me back—I am free to be who God has created me to be.
I DECLARE I was made to shine. My light is a gift, and I refuse to hide or shrink back—I will step forward with boldness.
I DECLARE I will not let fear or insecurity limit me. I walk with divine confidence, fully rooted in God's love and truth.
I DECLARE that what God has started in me, He will complete. I will stand strong, persevere, and boldly walk in my calling with full confidence.

ACTIVATE YOUR IMPACT

LOL ACTIVATION

Confidence is not just a feeling—it's a decision. A daily choice to believe what God says about you over what the world has tried to label you. It's time to silence the doubts, throw off every weight that has tried to hold you back, and walk boldly in who God created you to be.

You've just consumed the truth that activates your confidence. Now, it's time to take action. This is where true activation happens—when you stop hesitating and start showing up with confidence, knowing that God has already placed everything you need inside of you.

So let's do this. With bold faith, a heart wide open, and a commitment to walking in confidence, answer the following:

LEARN IT:

What labels or limiting beliefs have you carried that have held you back? Where have you doubted your confidence?

OWN IT:

What steps have you been avoiding because of fear or insecurity? Where have you been dimming your light instead of shining fully?

LIVE IT:

If you fully activated your confidence today—without hesitation, without fear—what would change? What is one bold action step you will take right now to move forward?

It's time to step up, stand firm, and *Live Out Loud* with unshakable confidence.

Chapter Four

ACTIVATE YOUR VISION

God's vision for your life isn't something you dream up—it's something He reveals. It's a glimpse of what already exists in Heaven, waiting for you to step into it.

Without vision, we drift. We hesitate. We second-guess. But when we see clearly, we move boldly.

> *"Where there is no vision, the people perish."*
> **(Proverbs 29:18, KJV)**

The enemy would love nothing more than for you to stay stuck, distracted, or overwhelmed by what you can't see. But God is calling you to walk by faith, not by sight. His vision for you is unfolding right on schedule.

You are not behind.
You have not missed it.
This is your appointed time.
You look exactly the way you're supposed to look.
You're the exact age you're supposed to be.

he way you're supposed to talk.
Question anything.

You were born to have this vision for this decade. Everything is on purpose, and everything is for your impact.

For years, I have prayed, *"God, give me eyes to see and ears to hear."* Vision requires revelation. We need to see what God is showing us and hear what He is saying.

GOD'S PATTERN FOR VISION IN SCRIPTURE

Vision is a divine assignment, not just an idea. There's a pattern we see over and over in the Bible:

1. God gives a vision.
2. There is a season of preparation.
3. The vision is fulfilled—on God's timeline.

Think about it:

- Joseph dreamed of leadership but spent years in slavery and prison before stepping into his calling.
- Moses was called to lead but spent 40 years in the wilderness before walking it out.
- David was anointed king long before taking the throne.
- Esther stepped into her divine assignment at exactly the right moment.
- Deborah led Israel with wisdom and courage in a time when it was unheard of for a woman to lead.

Each received a vision from God, but none of them walked into it overnight. They had to trust, wait, and stay obedient in the process.

ACTIVATE YOUR IMPACT

WHY VISION MATTERS IN BUSINESS & LIFE

Let's get real: Having vision means being unshakable—even on the hard days.

Your vision should be unbreakable. Not flexible. Not bendable. It should be as strong as steel so it won't bend on a bad day.

If you let discouragement, doubt, or outside opinions take the wheel, you'll drift. But if you stay locked in on the vision, no storm can knock you off course.

Remember, what you have created, *no one* can match because they are not you. They don't have your anointing for the same thing. And God does know your heart. Hold steady—He's bringing you to a higher vantage point.

Proverbs 29:18 tells us that without vision, people lose their way. But those who follow wisdom's guidance are blessed.

Jeremiah 17:7-8 gives us the key: *"But blessed is the one who trusts in the Lord, whose confidence is in him. They will be like a tree planted by the water that sends out its roots by the stream. It does not fear when heat comes; its leaves are always green. It has no worries in a year of drought and never fails to bear fruit"* (NIV).

> *When you have a clear vision, you are unshakable.*

Because here's the truth: Faith fuels vision. And as faith-driven women, we know God has good plans for us.

> *"For I know the plans I have for you, declares the Lord, plans to prosper you and not to harm you, plans to give you hope and a future."*
> **(Jeremiah 29:11, NIV)**

That's what I want you to hear: Hopeful expectation is how we live. Not wishful thinking. Faith-filled confidence.

In all seasons, I don't believe there is a finish line. The finish line keeps moving until the day we die. We will always have more growth, more expansion, more depth, more purpose, more pruning, more challenges, more success, more strength, and more courage. You will get the harvest—more fulfillment and more impact—whatever you allow!

Everything you are doing is for a purpose, and oftentimes, the next generation gets to step into the promise of what you are building right now. Is it worth it? Of course it is! Who is on the other side of your obedience to keep going and showing up anyway?

I recently saw a janitor late at night quietly tending to the plants with such excellence, even though no one was watching. His faithfulness in the small things spoke volumes—are we showing up with that same level of excellence, even when no one is watching?

One of the greatest lessons I have learned is this: If you don't know where you're going, you'll never get there. Vision keeps you moving forward, even when things don't make sense. It allows you to navigate seasons of waiting, pruning, and preparation.

I often talk about the four seasons we go through in life and business:

1. **Wilderness Seasons**—Times of spiritual isolation where it might seem as though God is silent or distant. You might feel lost, waiting for God to rescue you. In these times, you will need faith that God is true to His word.
2. **Pruning Seasons**—Times of purification, where God removes and strips away aspects of your life that do not contribute to your spiritual growth. You will need

faith that God is greater than any worldly thing or any loss you might feel.
3. **Growth Seasons**—Periods of stretching and testing when God pulls you out of your comfort zone and calls you to do something you've never done before. This is where FAITH comes in—relying on God's strength to carry you and growing with Him, realizing you are not meant to do it in your own strength.
4. **Harvest Seasons**—The reward for your obedience to God. This is when God grants the desires of your heart. However, even in this season, there are trials, and you will need faith not to turn your blessings into idols. You can't sow a seed without reaping a harvest —God is lining up your healing, breakthrough, and promotion. Keep being good to people. Keep planting good seeds.

The problem is that many people get stuck in one season and lose sight of where God is taking them next. Like Peter stepping out onto the water—when he kept his eyes on Jesus, he moved forward. When he looked at the waves, he began to sink.

"Vision is about focus. It's about keeping your eyes on Jesus and trusting that He is leading you from glory to glory."
(2 Corinthians 3:18)

SARA'S STORY

SHE COULDN'T SEE IT CLEARLY YET

Sara didn't come from a place of clarity.

She had vision—she always had. She was a driven, hard-working leader, always pushing to reach the top in every role she stepped into. But the environment she was in didn't support the fullness of what she was capable of.

Instead of encouragement, she faced skepticism. Instead of inspiration, she was surrounded by people who played small and questioned anyone who wanted more.

So, when she first stepped into *Live Out Loud*, she wasn't looking for vision—she was looking for clarity. She had the work ethic, the determination, the drive. But she didn't yet have the right surroundings to help her see what was truly possible.

But I did.

I remember standing in my kitchen with her, looking her in the eyes, and telling her something she had never heard spoken over her life: *There is more for you.*

She didn't fully believe it yet. But something in her shifted that day. She said yes to stepping into a room where women weren't afraid to dream big. Women who built, created, expanded—and brought each other with them.

During that first year, she didn't take massive action. Instead, she absorbed, listened, and started to see. That's when God began unlocking new levels in her life.

By year two, her vision had sharpened. She started walking in greater confidence. Opportunities opened—ones she never saw coming. She stepped into the fitness industry, and something clicked. She didn't just grow in business—she grew in faith.

Because when you activate vision, it doesn't just change what you see—it changes how you believe.

Her relationship with the Lord deepened. She saw His hand guiding every step, every opportunity, every breakthrough. She stopped questioning her worth and started walking boldly, knowing she was called.

Fast-forward to today: Sara owns her own fitness franchise and is still a top leader on the *Live Out Loud* team. She wakes up every morning knowing God's grace is new and confident in the calling He has placed on her life.

And she will never go back. That's what happens when vision is activated.

You don't shrink—you expand.

You don't question your worth—you own it.

You don't wait for permission—you walk in it.

Sara is proof that when you say yes to God's vision for your life, He will take you places you never imagined. He will unlock new levels. He will show you what's possible—if you're willing to believe.

REFLECT ON YOUR VISION

Take a moment to think about the next-level woman you desire to become. What does she value? What impact does she want to make in her business, personal life, faith, and community? Write this down in a few sentences and turn this vision into practical rules or habits.

You need a plan: Vision without strategy is just wishful thinking. Are you acting like it?

ACTIVATION 1: THIS IS YOUR APPOINTED TIME!

"Then the Lord answered me and said: Write the vision and make it plain on tablets, that he may run who reads it. For the vision is yet for an appointed time; but at the end, it will speak, and it will not lie. Though it tarries, wait for it; because it will surely come, it will not tarry."
(Habakkuk 2:2-3, NKJV)

God's vision for your life will be fulfilled in His perfect timing. Even if it feels like His promise is taking forever, it is right on schedule.

You are not behind. You have not missed your biggest opportunity. Even when God's plans and promises don't happen right away, He is working.

True progress requires patience. Each of these leaders had an unshakable conviction that God's vision would become reality. That conviction was the force and fire that kept them moving forward. The waiting wasn't wasted—it was preparation.

God's vision for your life isn't just about where you're going; it's about who you're becoming along the way. The process is producing His perfect work in you.

You are in the exact season you're meant to be in.

You were born for this moment.

You have been appointed for such a time as this.

God placed you here on purpose, for a purpose. Do not let desires for something "better," "shinier," or "easier" distract you from your destiny.

Declare Habakkuk 2:2-3 over your life today—God's vision for you is unfolding right on time. Speak it until your spirit aligns with the truth. Write down the vision He has placed in your heart for this decade.

Where is He leading you?

What has He already revealed?

The waiting is not a pause; it's preparation. Step into your appointed time with faith, knowing that even the smallest act of obedience activates the next level. You are exactly where you are meant to be. Trust His process, hold steady, and believe that He is positioning you for greater impact.

ACTIVATE YOUR IMPACT

ACTIVATION 2: INSTANT WISDOM

*"And if anyone longs to be wise,
ask God for wisdom, and he will give it!"*
(James 1:5, TPT)

Vision doesn't come from striving—it comes from revelation. And revelation requires wisdom.

If you want to build something that lasts, you need wisdom beyond what the world can offer. Wisdom to discern God's timing. Wisdom to navigate seasons of waiting and acceleration. Wisdom to recognize divine opportunities and shut out distractions. And that wisdom doesn't come from chasing every voice, opinion, or trend—it comes straight from the source: God Himself.

James 1:5 tells us that if we want wisdom, all we have to do is ask. That's it. No prerequisites. No waiting for the "right moment." No proving yourself first. Just ask, and He will give it.

Jeremiah 33:3 echoes this promise: *"Call to me and I will answer you and tell you great and unsearchable things you do not know."* God is waiting to download divine strategies into your life—clarity for your next step, vision for your future, and insight that no amount of research, networking, or hustle could ever match.

But here's the challenge: Are you asking Him first?

Too often, we seek clarity from the world instead of the Word. We second-guess our vision because of someone else's opinion. We scroll, we compare, we overanalyze—and before we know it, we've watered down what God originally spoke over us. But true vision doesn't come from looking around—it comes from looking up.

God's wisdom is the foundation for your vision. It cuts through confusion and aligns your steps with heaven's blueprint. It keeps you from chasing the wrong things and settling for less than what He has for you. It removes fear, doubt, and hesitation because when you walk in divine wisdom, you don't just hope—you KNOW.

God has already placed a vision inside you. But before you run with it, ask Him for wisdom to steward it well. Take a moment right now—pause, get still, and invite God to speak. Ask Him to reveal what you need to see, hear, and understand in this season.

Then, commit to making His voice your first source of wisdom. Before calling a friend, before taking a poll, before questioning what you already know—go to Him. Let His wisdom be the light that guides your vision. Because when you seek Him first, everything else becomes clear.

ACTIVATION 3: ACTIVATE YOUR HARVEST

"And don't allow yourselves to be weary in planting good seeds, for the season of reaping the wonderful harvest you've planted is coming! Take advantage of every opportunity to be a blessing to others, especially to our brothers and sisters in the family of faith!"
(Galatians 6:9-10, TPT)

The vision God has given you is already set in motion—but what you do with it determines the harvest you will see.

God's pattern is clear: He reveals the vision, and we partner with Him through faith and obedience. If you want to see that vision come to life, you have to plant seeds that align with it. Every word, decision, investment, and habit is a seed sown into your future.

So, here's the challenge: Are your daily seeds in agreement with the vision God has given you?

ACTIVATE YOUR IMPACT

If you don't like the harvest you're seeing in your life, look at what you've been planting. Are you sowing seeds of faith, obedience, and excellence? Or are you planting doubt, fear, and hesitation? Have you been nurturing what God has shown you, or have you let discouragement dry up the soil?

God never calls you to think small. In Mark 4:20, Jesus teaches us a Kingdom principle—when the Word of God (the ultimate seed) takes root in good soil, it produces a harvest 30, 60, or even 100 times what was planted.

That means when God gives you a vision, He is already preparing an overflowing harvest beyond what you could ask, think, or imagine. But here's the key—the size of the harvest is determined by how you steward the seed and where you plant it.

Not all soil produces a harvest. You cannot plant in places that drain you, distract you, or pull you away from God's purpose and expect to see Kingdom results. Your time, energy, and finances are all seeds, and they must be planted in soil that honors the Lord.

This means investing in businesses, relationships, and communities that align with God's vision. It means making sure your dollars are building something that glorifies the Kingdom. It means spending time on things that produce eternal impact, not just temporary gain.

A thirty-fold return is good, but why settle when God is offering more? A hundred-fold harvest is available but requires faith, diligence, and alignment. The difference isn't in God's ability—it's in your willingness to plant in the right places.

God will always do His part, but He won't do yours.

Farmers don't sit around waiting for crops to grow without first putting seed in the ground. They don't demand a harvest before they've planted. God brings the rain, the sunlight, and the supernatural increase—but it's on us to plant the seed, water it daily, and keep the weeds out.

Many people sit on God-given vision, waiting for perfect conditions. But faith doesn't wait—faith moves. Faith doesn't say, *I'll act when I see results.* Faith says, *I'll act because I see what God has shown me.*

When Jesus talked about bearing fruit in Matthew 7:16, He made it clear: *You will know them by their fruits.* Apple trees produce apples. Olive trees produce olives. You cannot expect a harvest of impact, influence, and Kingdom expansion if you are not sowing seeds of faith, obedience, and excellence every single day.

If you want to see the vision grow, you have to work the soil. Speak life over it. Steward it well. Stay faithful even when you don't see immediate results. Because God is not mocked—what you plant will grow.

Right now, take an honest inventory: What seeds have you been planting? What do your daily habits, words, and mindset say about the future you're creating? Are you investing in places that drain you, or are you planting in good soil that aligns with God's vision?

If anything is misaligned with the future you're believing for, shift today. Plant seeds that match the harvest you want to see. Speak faith. Act boldly. Align your daily actions with what God has shown you.

And don't grow weary—your season of reaping is coming. Keep sowing. Keep watering. Keep believing. The harvest is inevitable, and it will be greater than you ever imagined.

ACTIVATE YOUR IMPACT

SPEAK THIS OUT LOUD:

God, I trust that the vision You have placed inside of me is unfolding in Your perfect timing. I reject the lie that I am behind or that I have missed my moment. I declare that I am right where I am meant to be—positioned, prepared, and appointed for such a time as this. I refuse to let fear, doubt, or outside opinions cloud my vision. I will not shrink back. I will not second-guess. I will see what You are showing me, move in alignment with Your wisdom, and walk boldly in faith. My vision is not small—it is Kingdom-sized, and I will steward it well. I declare that as I plant good seeds and stay faithful in the process, my harvest is coming. My vision is activated, and I will walk it out with clarity, confidence, and conviction!

DECLARE YOUR VISION IS ACTIVATED

I DECLARE my vision is from God. He has appointed me for this time, and I will move forward in faith, knowing I am walking in His perfect plan.
I DECLARE I have divine wisdom and revelation. I do not move blindly—I seek God first, and He gives me clarity, strategy, and insight for every step.
I DECLARE I am committed to the process. I trust that every season—waiting, pruning, growing, and harvesting—is preparing me for greater impact.
I DECLARE I will plant seeds that align with my vision in good soil. I will sow faith, obedience, and excellence, knowing that my harvest will reflect what I have planted.
I DECLARE my vision is unstoppable. No fear, doubt, or distraction can keep me from stepping into what God has called me to do. I move boldly, expectantly, and with unwavering trust in His plan!

LOL ACTIVATION

You are not waiting for a vision—it has already been given to you. The question is, are you seeing it clearly, and are you walking in alignment with it?

Many people drift through life, allowing circumstances, distractions, or outside voices to blur what God has called them to do. But not you. Not anymore.

God has given you a vision. Now, it's time to take ownership of it.

What you see shapes what you believe.

What you believe determines how you move.

How you move will decide the impact you make.

This is where activation happens—when you stop questioning and start believing. When you stop hesitating and start stepping forward with confidence, knowing that God has already made a way.

So let's do this. With an open heart, bold faith, and a commitment to action, answer the following questions:

LEARN IT:

Where have you been unsure about your vision? Have you let doubt, fear, or outside opinions distort what God has already shown you?

ACTIVATE YOUR IMPACT

OWN IT:

What steps have you been avoiding because the vision feels too big? What distractions have kept you from fully stepping into what God has called you to do?

LIVE IT:

If you fully activated your vision today—without fear, without hesitation—what would change? What is one action step you will take right now to move forward?

Your vision is already in motion. Now, it's time to activate it.

SECTION 2: LIFE

Chapter Five

ACTIVATE YOUR CAPACITY

Capacity is about understanding what is truly possible—not just in the physical, but in the supernatural. When we talk about capacity from a biblical perspective, we are talking about what God can do through us when we align with Him and tap into His power.

BIBLICAL CAPACITY: EXPANDING WHAT'S POSSIBLE

The Bible is full of stories where God expanded people's capacity beyond what they thought was possible.

- **The Parable of the Talents (Matthew 25:14-30)**—This parable teaches us that when we steward well and take action, God entrusts us with more. Expansion comes to those who are faithful with what they've been given.

- **Peter Walks on Water (Matthew 14:22-33)**—Do you have the capacity to walk? Yes. But do you have the capacity to walk on water? Not without God. Peter didn't step out in his own ability—he stepped into supernatural capacity made possible by Jesus. Expansion requires faith to step into what only God can sustain.

- **Miraculous Conception in Old Age (Genesis 18:10-14, Luke 1:36-37)**—Sarah and Elizabeth both conceived in miraculous circumstances when it seemed impossible. God expanded their capacity to bear children, proving that nothing is too hard for Him. When He speaks expansion, He also provides the strength to carry it.

- **Everything You Need Is Already in You (2 Peter 1:3)**—God has already given you everything you need for life and godliness. Expansion isn't about striving—it's about recognizing what He has already provided and stepping into it with bold faith.

ROSHANDA'S STORY

WHEN GOD EXPANDS YOUR CAPACITY

Capacity isn't just about doing more. It's about *becoming more*. And often, the moments that stretch us the most start as simple acts of obedience.

I'll never forget when I first met Roshanda Pratt.

A mutual friend, Allison Andrews, introduced us and suggested she'd be a great guest for my podcast. At the time, I didn't know much about her, but I trusted Allison's recommendation. So, we set up the interview.

And what happened next?

God showed up.

We had an incredible conversation, but it wasn't just about business or visibility, which is one of Roshanda's specialties. Something deeper was happening.

Roshanda felt led to ask me about the Holy Spirit.

She had no idea about the prayers I had been quietly lifting up. She didn't know that I had been seeking God for clarity on my prayer language or that I was longing to understand what it meant to walk fully in the power of the Holy Spirit. She didn't know that just days later, I would be heading to a revival in Oregon, where I was praying for a deeper encounter with God.

But she listened to the prompting of the Holy Spirit. Instead of ignoring it or overthinking it, she obeyed.

After the podcast, she asked if we could stay on and continue to connect. I'm pretty sure neither of us really had the time or capacity for that in our schedules, but we both said yes to a miracle moment we didn't even know we were about to experience.

And then, she prayed over me.

She spoke words that confirmed what God had already been stirring in my heart. She encouraged me in a way that no one else could have in that moment. And as she prayed, I just started crying because I *knew* this was a divine appointment.

Her boldness unlocked something in me.

I had been intimidated by the prayer language I was craving, but her prayer gave me the confidence to embrace it. Through her, God revealed how tangible the Holy Spirit truly is. My Faith grew. My discernment deepened.

It created room for my understanding of the Holy Spirit and the capacity that was meant for me.

That is the most powerful part! Her obedience made room for a miracle moment that stretched her capacity for impact and *mine*.

From that day forward, we became more than acquaintances. More than business connections. More than women in the same circle. We became *family*.

And because of that moment, Roshanda became a part of *Live Out Loud* in ways I never could have imagined. She not only spoke on my stage in 2021—she became the emcee of my events for years after that. She became one of my best friends. She became someone I trust, love, and continue to do life with.

Roshanda didn't know that one act of obedience would unlock greater opportunities, stepping into an even *bigger* level of impact.

But that is exactly what happens when you allow God to expand your capacity.

So many people ask for greater influence, greater leadership, and greater platforms … but are unwilling to respond to the small promptings that make space for that expansion.

But here's the truth: Your next level is on the other side of your yes.

Roshanda wasn't looking for a lifelong friendship or more speaking opportunities. She wasn't trying to build her platform or expand her connections. She was simply being obedient. And because of that, God multiplied her impact—and mine.

So let me ask you: Where is God asking you to expand?

Is He calling you to step into a new opportunity, even if you don't feel ready? To stretch your leadership in a way that feels uncomfortable? To step out in faith when you don't have all the answers?

Because here's what I know—when you allow God to expand your capacity, when you make room for the miracle moments, He will *always* fill the space.

You don't have to force it. You just have to *say yes*.

ACTIVATE YOUR IMPACT

CAPACITY IS WORKING FROM OVERFLOW

Capacity isn't just about pushing harder—it's about alignment. It's about understanding what God has already given you and working from a place of overflow, not exhaustion. Too often, people think capacity means doing more, striving harder, or grinding endlessly.

Think of the famous story of the four-minute mile. For years, people believed it was physically impossible for a human to run a mile in under four minutes—until Roger Bannister did it in 1954.

Once that barrier was broken, many others followed. Why? Because belief shifted. Once people saw it was possible, they stepped into a new level of capacity.

The same is true for us. When we increase our belief in what is possible, we unlock new levels.

Can you think of a time in your life when something felt impossible, but then it actually happened? If not, know that your time is coming.

Expanding capacity starts with a choice. When I realized that no one was going to knock on my door and do my life for me—no one was going to build my faith, develop my relationships, grow my business, or take care of my health—I knew I had to make a decision. I had to decide to take responsibility for my *life*.

It's not about *feeling* like it—it's about what is possible. We cannot allow our emotions to dictate our life, our calendar, or our ability to reach our goals. People often say they want more energy, more peace, or more impact, but they don't decide to step into it because they don't "feel" like it.

What we believe is impossible in the natural is possible in the supernatural.

Philippians 4:13 says, *"I can do all things through Christ who strengthens me."* God is our source. We are limitless when we tap into the supernatural capacity He provides.

HOW I ACTIVATED MY CAPACITY DURING A SEASON OF UNCERTAINTY

My husband and I had been talking about moving our family across the country to live in our favorite place on earth: Newport Beach, California. It was a place we thought of as a magical fairyland with breathtaking landscapes and the bluest skies. For over a decade, we had also dreamed about Brett leaving his corporate job so that we could work together.

We had these conversations when our daughters were little, but now they were starting middle and high school. We knew if we didn't take the leap now, we might never do it.

We decided to burn the boats—leave everything we knew, everything that was safe, and take the risk. Brett left his 25-year career with the same company to go ALL IN with me.

So many people discouraged us, especially because of our ages. I was in my early 40s, and Brett was in his early 50s. We were told that no one does this at our stage of life.

We had already reached the pinnacle of success where we were, but it wasn't about success. It was about *the more* God had for us and the next level of capacity He was about to show us that only we could feel in our spirit. No one else could understand. We obeyed the call even though it didn't make sense to anyone.

I wish I could tell you that once we moved, everything fell into place seamlessly. However, what we stepped into was not just a new home or a new business venture—it was the beginning of a complete awakening. A rebirth. A renewal. A revival of everything we were made for with God.

Just six months later ... COVID hit.

We were in California, and suddenly, the world shut down. The dreams we had pursued and the risks we had taken all felt like they were hanging in the balance. But we didn't run back.

There was nothing to run back to. We knew we had to make it work.

This was a defining moment, a season of testing and refining. It would have been easier to go back, to lean on the comfort of familiarity, or even to retreat to family. But we knew we had a calling, and we had to be obedient to it, so we took action anyway.

Most people would have stopped, given up, and gone back. But we chose a different path. We stepped into supernatural capacity, and God multiplied it beyond anything we could have imagined.

When the world shut down, I could feel the uncertainty, the fear, and the panic all around me. But I already knew what it was like to go down a dark, long road of discouragement and despair. I had been there before when I received my cancer diagnosis. And I **knew** that was not my portion.

I prayed for supernatural hope, confidence, and security—for the ability to step into what we were called to do. While everyone else was stagnant and depressed … I had hope!

Instead of shutting down, I showed up. I started growing my online business, expanding my network marketing team, and launching my podcast. I refused to let fear dictate my actions. Instead, I activated my faith, business, habits, network, and skills—what I now call my *Activation System*.

Every morning, I prayed specific prayers:

- *God, give me supernatural energy.*
- *God, help me operate from overflow.*
- *God, increase my capacity so I can serve and lead well.*

That season expanded my belief in what was possible. I realized that supernatural capacity is not about striving—it's about surrendering and stepping into what God has already prepared for us.

BROOKE THOMAS
LIVE — OUT — LOUD

THE ACTIVATION SYSTEM

ACTIVATE YOUR **FAITH** | ACTIVATE YOUR **HABITS** | ACTIVATE YOUR **NETWORK** | ACTIVATE YOUR **SKILLS** | ACTIVATE YOUR **BUSINESS**

REPLENISHING CAPACITY

Supernatural energy doesn't come from overworking; it comes from being filled up. When my energy starts to drain, I take intentional steps to replenish it:

- I turn on worship music and let it shift my atmosphere. Worship always drowns out worry and fuels my energy.
- I pray out loud in my atmosphere over my mind and body. I go on a walk and place my hand on my heart, repeating, *"God, I know You've got me,"* and *"You've got this."* This allows me to reset my nervous system and renew my capacity.
- I declare scripture out loud. It is living and breathing and will always refresh your soul.

ACTIVATE YOUR IMPACT

- I use my voice to speak out the opposite of any negative emotions. For example, if I feel fear, I tell it to go! If I feel intimidated, I tell intimidation to leave me alone.

We are spiritual beings, and we choose what we receive and what we reject.

When we invite God into our daily routine, we access a supernatural strength that cannot be explained.

ACTIVATION 1: SUPERNATURAL ENERGY

"Are you tired? Worn out? Burned out on religion? Come to me. Get away with me and you'll recover your life. I'll show you how to take a real rest. Walk with me and work with me—watch how I do it. Learn the unforced rhythms of grace. I won't lay anything heavy or ill-fitting on you. Keep company with me and you'll learn to live freely and lightly."
(Matthew 11:28, MSG)

People always comment on my energy. Do you want to know my secret? It's in this scripture!

I learned a long time ago to pray before bed: *"God, wake me up with supernatural energy!"* I believe that He will, and He does!

I also have learned to stop and get refreshed with worship music or talking with God whenever I feel tired, stressed, or worn down throughout the day. He always refreshes my spirit!

We all need daily refreshing—time and space to recenter so we can continue to pursue our passions and show up for our people rested and revitalized. But did you hear what Jesus says? *"Come to me. Get away with me and you'll recover your life."*

When you're at the end of your rope, *come to Me.*
When you're exhausted as soon as you wake, *come to Me.*
When you have nothing left to give, *come to Me.*
When you need to get away from it all, *come to Me.*

When you pursue Jesus, a different kind of refreshing happens—a refreshing that lasts far beyond the five-minute break or weekend getaway. Jesus doesn't invite you into rest and peace every now and again, He invites you to rest with Him every single day. This is how your capacity expands.

He PROMISES you can "learn the unforced rhythms of grace." Isn't that so powerful? Instead of a daily grind, you can have a rhythm of grace. All you have to do is watch how He does it!

… recovery
… rest
… rejuvenation
… freedom
… relief from the heavy burdens

Today, spend some time with the Lord—not out of obligation, not to check off a task, but because it's the most life-giving, energizing thing you could ever do.

Can you set aside the distractions, the pressures, and the endless to-do list and simply rest in His presence? Let His words wash over you—freely and lightly. DECLARE this truth: The real secret to a better, more powerful, more productive day is always Jesus.

I've found that when I devote time to the Lord, He expands my capacity. He multiplies my time, giving me the ability to accomplish more for His Kingdom. God expands time. He always does. Reading His Word fuels me. It strengthens me. It makes me more of who He's called me to be.

As a high-achieving, high-performing woman, my brain and my flesh often resist this truth. It doesn't make sense in the natural—there has never been a time when I chose to trade it out for something else, and it worked.

That's why it's supernatural. It defies logic. It won't ever make sense to our minds. But God doesn't work in the natural— He works in the supernatural. And that's exactly where we're called to operate.

ACTIVATION 2: THE POWER OF ENDURANCE

> *"My fellow believers, when it seems as though you are facing nothing but difficulties, see it as an invaluable opportunity to experience the greatest joy that you can! For you know that when your faith is tested it stirs up in you the power of endurance."*
> **(James 1:2-3, TPT)**

Endurance is a superpower all of God's daughters need! When you are going all in with Jesus, life can feel exactly like James said: "Facing nothing but difficulties." This is why I believe God wants to activate the power of endurance in you!

Endurance from God gives us the power to smile at our trials! To live in joy even when we're surrounded by chaos.

I KNOW there's a real enemy trying to wear us down. We're running our race in a world constantly trying to trip us up, wear us down, and take us out. But God has gifts for us: dunamis strength, bold faith, unshakable confidence, perfect joy, extravagant love, and supernatural capacity!

Let's pause for a second to reframe the really hard stuff that's going on in your life. James tells us to see them as invaluable opportunities to experience joy.

What makes you so exhausted that you're unsure you can take another step?

Where does it feel like life is beating you down?

Where do you feel stuck?

Where is your hope starting to flicker?

What do you feel like you don't have capacity for?

Name every obstacle. Each allows God to stretch your capacity and empower you with divine endurance. Now believe that the power is already inside of you, just waiting to be stirred up!

So take a deep breath, stand firm, and declare: I will not back down—I am stepping into the endurance, strength, and capacity God has already placed inside of me!

ACTIVATION 3: EXPAND MY TERRITORY!

"He was the one who prayed to the God of Israel,
'Oh, that you would bless me and expand my territory!
Please be with me in all that I do, and keep me from all
trouble and pain!' And God granted him his request."
(1 Chronicles 4:10, NLT)

Jabez didn't hold back—he boldly asked God to bless him and expand his territory. And do you know how God responded? He said yes!

This scripture changed everything for me. It gave me permission to pray for myself first, not just for others. Many people don't think they can do that, but this verse taught me I can. Like an oxygen mask on a plane, you can't help others if you're not breathing first. I needed to pray for my own expansion so I could be a greater blessing to others.

Then the expansion piece hit me. I started boldly praying over my business. Over my network. Over my influence.

I began declaring: "Lord, bring people from the north, south, east, and west. Expand my reach beyond what I can see. Stretch my capacity to hold more of what You have for me!"

And guess what? He did it. Because I asked for expansion, God started sending global connections. He multiplied my impact, and He gave me the capacity to handle it.

So now it's your turn. It's time to ask boldly and believe for more. *God, expand my territory beyond what I can see. Increase my capacity to lead and steward well. Expand my business, my network, and my influence so that I can be a greater blessing for Your Kingdom. Bring the right people into my life from the north, south, east, and west. Be with me, protect me, and work through me in every step I take. I am asking, I am believing, and I am ready to receive the expansion You have for me.*

When we boldly ask for expansion, God doesn't just give us more—He gives us the strength, wisdom, and capacity to sustain it. That's the whole point!

We serve a God who makes the impossible possible every single day. Now, ask and declare—He's ready to expand YOU!

SPEAK THIS OUT LOUD:

God, I trust You as my Source. I refuse to believe the lie that I am not capable. I declare that I am created in Your image—with supernatural strength, wisdom, and capacity. I will not shrink back. I will not let limitations define me. I will step boldly into the expansion You have for me, knowing that You have already equipped me. My capacity is not lacking—it is waiting to be activated. I release fear, doubt, and hesitation, and I embrace the strength and endurance You have placed inside of me. I am ready. I am expanding. I am stepping into more for Your glory!

DECLARE YOUR CAPACITY IS ACTIVATED

I DECLARE God has given me the capacity to hold more. I will no longer operate from a place of lack—I have everything I need to sustain the expansion He has for me!
I DECLARE my endurance is supernatural. I will not grow weary or back down. What God has called me to, He will equip me to handle!
I DECLARE I am stepping into divine expansion. I am ready for new opportunities, greater influence, and increased impact.
I DECLARE fear and doubt have no hold on me. I refuse to limit myself based on what I think I can handle—I trust God to stretch and strengthen me!
I DECLARE I will steward my expansion well. I will lead with wisdom, build with excellence, and walk in obedience to God's plans!

ACTIVATE YOUR IMPACT

LOL ACTIVATION

Your capacity is not fixed—it is waiting to be expanded. Too often, people believe they can only handle what they've always handled. They assume they have reached their limit. Not you. Not anymore.

You've just consumed truth that ignites your capacity. Now, it's time to step into expansion.

What you believe about your limits will determine what you step into.

What you step into will determine what you steward.

And what you steward will determine how God expands you next.

This is where activation happens—when you stop questioning whether you can handle more and start declaring that God has already given you the capacity to rise.

So let's do this. With an open heart, bold faith, and a commitment to action, answer the following questions:

LEARN IT:

Where have you believed the lie that you are at your limit? Where have you hesitated to ask God for more?

OWN IT:

What area of your life is God calling you to expand? What next level are you resisting because it feels too big?

LIVE IT:

If you fully stepped into your God-given capacity today—without fear, without hesitation—what would change? What is one action step you will take right now to move forward?

Chapter Six

ACTIVATE YOUR RELATIONSHIPS

Relationships are the foundation of everything I've built. They are the lifeblood of my success, my community, and the impact I've been able to make in this world. But relationships aren't just about business—they are about life itself. We were created for connection, designed to live in relationship with others.

And as believers, relationships are even more important.

God didn't design us to build alone. We are called to community—to encourage, refine, and activate one another. Proverbs 27:17 says, *"As iron sharpens iron, so one person sharpens another."*

The right relationships don't just support you, they stretch you, strengthen you, and call out the gifts God has placed inside of you.

But here's the thing: Relationships don't grow in isolation. They need to be nurtured. They need to be activated. And the best place for that to happen is within a strong, faith-filled community.

I remember a time when I was searching for a community like this—one that was bold in faith and big in vision. A space where women could talk about building wealth and building the Kingdom in the same conversation. A sisterhood that called each other higher.

But no matter where I looked, I couldn't find it.

So I prayed.

I asked God to show me where to go, who to connect with, and what room I needed to be in. And I'll never forget what He told me: "Go create it."

That was the moment *Live Out Loud* was born—not as a business strategy, but as an act of obedience.

From the very beginning, I knew this had to be more than just a network or a mastermind. It had to be a movement: a place where women could step fully into their God-given callings, lead with integrity, and build businesses that didn't just create wealth but expanded the Kingdom of God.

That's why finding the *right* community is so important.

The truth is, we were never meant to do this alone. We need people around us who won't just agree with us but will push us, pray for us, and remind us of the bigger vision. The kind of people who don't just cheer for our success but fight for our growth.

So let me ask you: How are your relationships doing?

Many people only think about relationships when they break down. Maybe a betrayal left a scar, or a misunderstanding created distance. But relationships aren't just something to manage when they go wrong; they are something to activate, nurture, and build intentionally. Because the right relationships don't just support you—they *activate* you. They challenge you to grow, push you toward purpose, and open doors you could never walk through alone.

Here's the truth: Not every relationship is meant to go where you're going. And not every relationship can be activated in the same way.

THE *LIVE OUT LOUD* COMMUNITY: BUILT ON TRUST & INTEGRITY

My faith has shaped how I build relationships and nurture the *Live Out Loud* community. Who you surround yourself with matters. You are the people you spend time with. When I started this community, I knew we needed to set a standard for relationships—a culture of integrity, trust, and collaboration.

Psalm 15:2-5 (TPT) perfectly describes what this looks like:

They are passionate and wholehearted, always sincere and always speaking the truth— for their hearts are trustworthy. They refuse to slander or insult others; they'll never listen to gossip or rumors, nor would they ever harm a friend with their words. They will despise evil and evil workers while commending the faithful ones who follow after the truth. They make firm commitments and follow through, even at great cost. They never crush others with exploitation, and they would never be bought with a bribe against the innocent. Those who do these things will never be shaken; they will stand firm forever.

This is the foundation we live by. This community has a zero-tolerance policy for jealousy, offense, and gossip.

I have said this in every business I've built from the very beginning: If you have it, release it.

Anything that causes division—offense, jealousy, gossip—destroys relationships, businesses, and communities faster than anything else. I've learned that the best way to guard against division is to be self-aware before reacting.

Early in my journey, I used to respond quickly to things that offended me. But I've learned that true strength and leadership come from pausing, reflecting, and inviting God into those moments. When something stirs up offense in me, I ask:

Why do I feel this way?
What in me needs to be healed or strengthened?
What lesson is God trying to teach me through this?

Trust me, this has been really hard for me. But over time, I've learned that it has been the most rewarding thing to do.

It's so easy to let assumptions and emotions take over. But the most mature thing we can do—especially as women in business and community—is to pause. Don't let the enemy build a case against someone in your heart when it could actually be an opportunity for growth and leadership.

This requires self-control. It requires leaning on the Holy Spirit. And it requires trusting that God's ultimate desire is restoration and unity, not division.

When I feel hurt or offended, I've learned to take it to the Lord first. Because if I respond from a place of wisdom rather than reaction, I can protect the relationships God has placed in my life.

So my challenge to you is this: *Be a leader who pauses.* Instead of reacting, let God refine you. When we remove the things that divide us, we make room for relationships that activate us. That's where true community and kingdom impact happen.

ACTIVATE YOUR IMPACT

KATIE'S STORY

FROM ISOLATION TO ACTIVATION

I still remember the moment I first connected with Katie. She had seen something on my Instagram story about an event I was hosting at The Ritz, Laguna Niguel, and sent me a DM that simply said: "Just tell me how to sign up."

I didn't know her at all but could feel her urgency. She wasn't just interested—she knew in her spirit that she needed to be in that room. So, I asked if we could have a phone conversation.

We laughed about how we got our hair done at the same place, talked about where she was in life, and as I started explaining what the event was all about, she interrupted me and said, "I don't even care what it is. I just know I need to be there."

I could hear it in her voice—she wasn't just looking for another event or networking opportunity. She was searching for something more.

It wasn't until later that she told me what was really happening behind the scenes.

A week before she sent that DM, Katie had been in her bedroom, tearfully praying for connection. She had moved to a new state with her family eight months earlier and was struggling to find real friendships. She had always been the kind of woman who could connect with anyone, but for some reason, this transition felt different.

That day, she cried out to God: "Lord, I don't know if I can keep doing this. I feel so alone."

And in the stillness, she heard Him whisper, "Be patient. There's more."

More came just six days later, when she found herself in a parking lot on the phone with me, stepping into something she didn't fully understand yet.

That first event at The Ritz, Laguna Niguel, was small—just 15 women—but something came alive in Katie that day. She felt seen. She felt connected. She felt like she had found her people. When she stood up to speak, she realized how much she had missed being in an environment that called her higher.

She joined the *Live Out Loud* business network and spent the next three years deeply investing in the community. Even through 2020, when everything felt uncertain, she stayed locked in. We prayed together, encouraged each other, and continued moving forward.

But her journey didn't stop there.

Over time, we became more than just business connections—we became family. Our kids started hanging out, we had karaoke nights, and before we knew it, we had built a bond that neither of us expected. Today, Katie is not only one of my best friends, but she's now a key part of the *Live Out Loud* team.

Here's the thing: Katie talks about this community all the time. She shares her experience constantly, and because of her, so many women have found their way into this movement. She is one of the biggest reasons new women continue to come into *Live Out Loud*—when something changes your life, you can't help but share it.

She always says, "I met my best friend at 40, so there's still hope for you!" And she's right—sometimes, when you feel the most alone or think it's too late to find your people, God is setting you up for something greater than you could ever ask or imagine.

All He needs is for you to believe in it—and take that first step.

ACTIVATE YOUR IMPACT

DIVINE RELATIONSHIPS: GOD-ORDAINED CONNECTIONS

I believe relationships, partnerships, and collaborations are meant to be under the Kingdom of God. There's a divine principle at work that goes beyond human understanding.

There are people God sends into your life for a reason. These divine relationships will take you to levels you never could have reached on your own. They come into your life with no selfish agenda—only obedience to what God has called them to do.

I didn't fully understand the power of divine relationships until I experienced one in a way I could never deny.

I had just experienced a spiritual breakthrough—a freedom session that changed my life. At the time, my daughters were just two and five years old, and I had been set free from things I didn't even realize I was carrying—generational strongholds like fear and intimidation that had been keeping me from stepping fully into my calling.

Not long after that experience, I was invited to speak at an event in California. It was a huge opportunity, but as I got on the plane, I kept asking God, *Was that real? Did I really break free from fear and intimidation? Was my voice really going to be strong and heard? Or was it just a glimpse of what I desired?*

I didn't tell anyone about this internal battle. I just kept praying, asking God for confirmation.

As soon as I arrived at the event, an older woman walked straight up to me and asked, "Are you a believer?"

I laughed. *I have been talking to God this entire way here.*

She told me she wasn't even supposed to be at this event. She and her husband had traveled from Boston, but when I walked through the door, she immediately knew why God had brought her there. She told me that she saw a vision of me running through a finish line with a yellow ribbon, like I had just won a race.

Then she looked me in the eye and said, "God wants you to know that you have experienced victory and freedom. You just finished a race, and the victory is yours."

At that moment, I *knew* God was speaking to me. He sent this woman across the country to confirm what I had been praying for.

Over the next several days, she prayed with me, encouraged me, and spoke words over my life that only God could have given her. She reminded me how seen, loved, and cared for I was by God. I wrote down everything she said, carrying those words with me for years as I confidently stepped into my calling.

One specific prayer she prayed over me became my anthem: *"Rise up, woman of God! This is your time! No more fear! No more shame! This is your moment! You were made for this! Go speak!"*

Every time I stepped on a stage to speak, I carried those words with me.

That relationship didn't end after that event. She stayed in my life for years, praying over me and encouraging me, expecting nothing in return. She was a divine connection.

From that moment forward, I *knew* that divine relationships were real.

Since then, there have been too many stories to count of how good God has been to send me the most incredible, divine relationships. Some have become my lifelong friends—people who feel like family. Others have been placed in my life for a season, but their impact has been undeniable.

One of the most incredible stories of divine connection happened in early 2024 at my *Live Out Loud* retreat at the Ritz-Carlton, Laguna Niguel.

Just as my retreat was beginning, I experienced one of the deepest betrayals of my life—something only a handful of people knew about. Someone I loved and trusted betrayed me. She had been trying to divide my community and tear down what God had built. I had no idea what was happening behind the scenes until my closest friends and team members told me.

Just a few hours after hearing the news, one of my close friends brought over a woman who had been looking for me. Her name was Caroline. She was from Germany, and she had a thank-you card in her hands.

She had been following me for years on social media. (I guess social media really does work!) She was flying home to Germany but had a layover in Los Angeles. When she realized that our event was happening nearby, she left the airport and came *just* to deliver this card and say thank you.

She found one of my best friends, whom she recognized from following me online, and asked if she could pass along the card. But instead of just delivering it, my friend walked her straight over to me.

Caroline stood in front of me with tears in her eyes and said, "Thank you for cheering me on across the world! For believing in me when no one else did. I just wanted to say thank you."

She went on to tell me that when no one else believed in her ideas, she prayed and asked God to send her someone. And somehow, through social media, she found *me*, and I had been that encouragement.

She had no idea what I was going through that day. She had no idea that my heart was breaking. But God *did*. He sent her at that exact moment to remind me that He is in control.

My closest friends stood around in awe of how perfectly God orchestrates everything.

That night, I had to lead people into *Encounter Night* while betrayal was heavy on my mind. But everything shifted when she walked up to me and shared her story. She had no agenda. She expected nothing. She just wanted to say thank you.

I invited her to stay for *Encounter Night*. We gave her *Live Out Loud* gear, and she fully stepped into the experience.

That night, a few women from the community invited her to

church with them. She went the next morning—and in a moment she never expected, she accepted Jesus as her Lord and Savior.

And before she got back on a plane to Germany, she was baptized.

She left that retreat fully decked out in *Live Out Loud* gear, saved, renewed, and forever changed.

She stayed in touch, became a member of our community, and eventually joined our mastermind. She became our first international member, just as I had received a prophecy years before that *Live Out Loud* would go global.

That moment was a clear representation of how God moves.

> *"And we know that in all things God works for the good of those who love Him, who have been called according to His purpose."*
> **(Romans 8:28, NIV)**

The enemy had sent betrayal. But God sent *divine restoration*.

More than a decade after my first divine encounter, He still shows me the power of divine relationships.

That's how it's *supposed* to work in the Kingdom of God.

When God prompts you to encourage someone, do it right then.

When He puts it on your heart to pray for someone, pray for them right then.

When you feel led to do something for someone, say it right then.

Because divine relationships aren't just about what we receive, they're about what we're willing to give.

ACTIVATE YOUR IMPACT

THE GIFT OF CONNECTION: BE THE ONE WHO BRINGS PEOPLE TOGETHER

I'm known as a super-connector for a reason. It's not because I'm the loudest in the room or know everyone—it's because I *see* people. I see their purpose, their potential, and who they're meant to be connected to. And I act on it.

I truly believe that when God can trust you with your heart and His people, He brings you more. More relationships. More opportunities. More influence. Because He knows you won't gatekeep. He knows you'll bring people together for the right reasons.

That's how I've built the *Live Out Loud* community—not through strategy, but through stewardship.

I've watched what happens when people hold on too tightly—afraid that promoting someone else will somehow take away from their own success.

But that's not how the Kingdom works. God doesn't operate in scarcity. We serve an extravagant God who multiplies what we're willing to *give away*.

I believe in promoting others. I believe in championing women behind their backs—in the best way possible. When you become someone who connects and celebrates others, *God will give you more people to lead*.

Relationship equity is the *best* equity. Women who are considering joining the *Live Out Loud* community often ask, "What's the return on my investment?" I remind them that the ROI here isn't just financial; it's also relational, spiritual, and generational.

The seeds you plant in this space will grow long after the season you're in. I've watched connections in this community turn into lifelong friendships, business partnerships, speaking opportunities, podcast features, book deals, and new revenue streams that continue to multiply for years to come.

And now, we've gone global. Connections are happening around the world because people have caught the vision. The relationships are the real return.

But here's the thing: this isn't just something that *happens*. Being a connector is a *muscle*—you have to train it. You have to stay awake to where you've been, who helped you get there, and who you're being called to lift up.

So, when you walk into a room, pause and ask:

Who can I connect in here?

Who needs to meet someone I know?

Who can I talk about in the best way today?

Steward your relationships well. Honor the people around you. Stay rooted in trust, and God will keep bringing you the right people for the next level.

Be a connector. Activate this. Choose to do this.

THE POWER OF NETWORKING: RELATIONSHIPS ACCELERATE SUCCESS

In both business and life, the fastest way to grow, expand, and make an impact is through relationships.

No skill will open doors faster than knowing the right people, connecting with the right people, being in the right rooms, and having the right introductions. Relationships will accelerate your success more than any talent or resource you have.

Here's why: Trust speeds up everything.

When you are in a room where trust is already built, that trust extends to you. Business happens faster. Opportunities come easier. Growth accelerates. I see this happening all the time inside the *Live Out Loud* community—women connecting, collaborating, and activating each other's success.

I've built my business this way.

The level of relationships in my world is never surface level

—it's always about going deeper, faster. When I talk about networking, I'm not just talking about attending events and exchanging business cards. I've never been excited about surface-level conversations. What I value—and what truly creates impact—is deep, meaningful, long-term relationships.

That's why I teach the *Honor Matrix*.

THE HONOR MATRIX: ELEVATING EVERY RELATIONSHIP

Honor is the fastest way to activate relationships. It unlocks trust, deepens connection, and attracts the right people into your life. If you want to grow in leadership, business, or influence, start with honor.

But let me be clear: Honor isn't just about respecting authority. It's about creating a culture of integrity that flows in every direction. That's why I teach the Honor Matrix—a framework for honoring in three key areas of your life:

- **Honor Up**—Honor those ahead of you.
- **Honor Down**—Honor those who serve and support you.
- **Honor All The Way Around**—Honor your peers and those beside you.

When you master this, you'll activate relationships that take you further than skill, knowledge, or strategy ever could.

THE HONOR MATRIX

Honor Up: Learn From Those Ahead of You

Honoring up means respecting and learning from those ahead of you—your mentors, leaders, and decision-makers. Too often, people try to prove they don't need help instead of recognizing that God places people ahead of us to guide us.

You can struggle alone, or you can humble yourself and learn from those who have already walked the path. Honoring up looks like seeking wisdom instead of trying to impress, expressing gratitude, and publicly celebrating the people who have paved the way for you.

Honor Down: Value Those Who Serve and Support You

Honor down is just as important. True leaders don't just demand honor—they give it.

This means valuing and appreciating those who serve and support you—your team, clients, assistants, service providers, and even the unseen workers who make things happen behind the scenes. I have seen people lose favor simply because they treated others poorly.

You can impress leaders all day long, but if you dishonor those who work with and for you, it will always come back

ACTIVATE YOUR IMPACT

around. God promotes those who serve with integrity. Never be too important to acknowledge and appreciate the people who make your vision possible.

Honor All The Way Around: Choose Collaboration Over Competition

Honor all the way around is where most people struggle.

It's easy to honor those above us and those below us, but what about the people running the same race as you? What about the ones you compare yourself to?

If you truly want to activate your relationships, you must learn to honor your peers—even your competitors. Celebrate their wins, speak life over them, and choose collaboration over competition. When you honor those around you, you create a culture of abundance, connection, and trust.

And trust always leads to favor.

So here's my challenge: For the next 90 days, honor three people daily—one mentor, one team member or supporter, and one peer. When you make honor a habit, you will attract divine connections, accelerate your influence, and open doors that no skill or strategy could open. Honor is a Kingdom principle, and when you activate honor, God activates favor.

ACTIVATION 1: YOU'RE NOT MEANT TO BUILD ALONE

*"For the body does not consist of one part, but of many ...
But now, God has arranged the parts, each one
of them in the body, just as He desired."*
(1 Corinthians 12:14-18, AMP)

God never designed us to build alone. The Body of Christ isn't just a concept for the church—it's a blueprint for how we operate in every area of life, including business.

We are co-laborers with Christ, and He strategically places the right people in our lives at the right time. Some to lead. Some to support. Some to finance. Some to build. But when we come together in unity, we expand the Kingdom in ways we never could alone.

I see this happen all the time inside *Live Out Loud*.

- At events, women pray together, release strongholds, and form Kingdom collaborations.
- On mastermind calls, they challenge each other in business, share strategies, and refine their leadership.
- At retreats, they rest, recharge, and receive fresh vision for their next level.

And then? They go back into their businesses, and the impact multiplies.

- They pray for one another.
- They refer business to one another.
- They finance Kingdom projects together.
- They activate new opportunities and build influence.

This is how Kingdom relationships work.

ACTIVATE YOUR IMPACT

So ask yourself:

- Am I building alone or alongside other Kingdom-minded leaders?
- Am I stewarding my role in the Body of Christ, or am I trying to do it all myself?
- Am I aligned with people who sharpen me, challenge me, and activate my next level?

If you've been feeling stuck, disconnected, or carrying too much on your own, this is your invitation to step into true Kingdom collaboration.

You weren't meant to do this alone. Get in the right room.

Step in. Connect. Build.

Activation 2: Keep Growing!

> *"How enriched are they who find their strength in the Lord; within their hearts are the highways of holiness! Even when their paths wind through the dark valley of tears, they dig deep to find a pleasant pool where others find only pain. He gives to them a brook of blessing filled from the rain of an outpouring. They grow stronger and stronger with every step forward, and the God of all gods will appear before them in Zion."*
> **(Psalm 84:5-7, TPT)**

Relationships require growth. And growth isn't always easy.

Let's be real—there will be moments in your relationships where you feel disappointed, misunderstood, or even hurt. Maybe you've experienced betrayal. Maybe you've outgrown certain connections. Maybe you're walking through a season where it feels like no one truly sees or supports you.

But here's what I know: You don't quit. You KEEP GROWING.

You can choose to sit in the pain, replay the hurt, and let it make you bitter *or* you can press in, dig deeper, and allow God to refine you through the relationships He places in your life.

I know you're an option #2 kind of woman. You know that growth—real, lasting growth—happens in relationships. It happens when you choose forgiveness over offense. When you choose honor over resentment. When you choose to surround yourself with people who call you higher, even when it challenges you.

Psalm 84:5-7 isn't just a poetic passage—it's a roadmap for how to grow in relationships.

- When you feel the sting of disappointment, dig deep into God's strength instead of reacting in emotion.
- When someone walks away, trust that God is making room for divine connections.
- When relationships challenge you, embrace the refining process instead of resisting it.

This is your invitation to keep growing in your relationships.

Listen, it might not feel the way you think it will. Growth isn't always comfortable. Godly relationships require godly character. Integrity is costly. It takes work to build a strong, healthy, Kingdom-aligned network.

But here's what I know for sure: when you choose to grow in your relationships, God expands your capacity for connection, influence, and impact.

So, when it feels like relationships are testing you, remember that you are being refined, not rejected. You are being strengthened, not sidelined.

Keep growing.

Because on the other side of this season? Divine relationships. Favor. Expansion. And the exact people God has assigned to walk with you into your next level.

ACTIVATE YOUR IMPACT

SPEAK THIS OUT LOUD:

God, I thank You for the relationships You have placed in my life. I refuse to believe the lie that I have to build alone. I declare that I am positioned in the right place, with the right people, for the right purpose. I will not shrink back in isolation. I will step forward in bold faith, knowing that You have designed me for Kingdom relationships, divine connections, and supernatural expansion. I release past disappointments, betrayals, and fears and embrace the people You have called to walk alongside me. My relationships are protected, strengthened, and activated for Your glory.

DECLARE YOUR RELATIONSHIPS ARE ACTIVATED

I DECLARE I am designed for connection. God has placed me in a Kingdom community where I will grow, thrive, and multiply my impact.

I DECLARE that divine relationships are aligning for my next level. God is bringing the right people into my life at the right time.

I DECLARE that offense, jealousy, and division have no place in my relationships. I choose honor, trust, and collaboration.

I DECLARE that I will build in faith, not in fear. I will not let past betrayals keep me from stepping into new, God-ordained relationships.

I DECLARE that I am a person of integrity, trust, and honor. I attract Kingdom-minded leaders, visionaries, and builders who push me toward my God-given purpose.

LOL ACTIVATION

You were created for community, but have you fully activated it?

Too many people walk through life believing they have to do everything alone. They have been hurt before, so they hesitate to trust again. They desire deep, meaningful connections, but fear has kept them guarded. Not anymore.

You have just received the truth about the power of divine relationships. Now, it is time to take action.

What you consume is what you believe.

What you believe is what you speak.

What you speak is what you live out.

This is where activation happens—when you stop hesitating, doubting, or isolating and start stepping into the community, connections, and relationships God has prepared for you.

So let's do this. With an open heart, bold faith, and a commitment to action, answer the following questions:

LEARN IT:

Where have you been isolating yourself in business or relationships? What fears or past wounds have held you back from fully trusting and collaborating?

ACTIVATE YOUR IMPACT

OWN IT:

What Kingdom relationships do you need to activate? Who do you need to reach out to, support, or honor?

LIVE IT:

If you fully embraced Kingdom community today—without hesitation, without fear—what would change? What is one action step you will take right now to build, connect, or restore a relationship?

Chapter Seven

ACTIVATE YOUR LEGACY

What will you leave behind?

This chapter is not about money, real estate, or businesses passed down. This is about something far greater: the eternal impact you make with your life. The ripple effect of your obedience. The lives you touch. The Kingdom you build.

Legacy is not just what you leave for others; it's what you leave IN others. It's the mark of a life lived fully in purpose, boldly in faith, and intentionally in action.

Here's what you need to understand: *legacy is not automatic.* It's a choice. You either build it, or you don't. And that choice is made every single day in how you show up, lead, give, and steward what God has placed in your hands.

WHAT LEGACY REALLY MEANS

Legacy is not about *you*—it's about what God does *through you*. It's about how your faith, leadership, and impact continue long after you're gone. It's the spiritual inheritance you leave for the next generation.

The Bible makes this clear:

- "*A good person leaves an inheritance for their children's children ...*" (Proverbs 13:22).
- "*His offspring will be mighty in the land; the generation of the upright will be blessed*" (Psalm 112:2).
- "*But the plans of the Lord stand firm forever, the purposes of his heart through all generations*" (Psalm 33:11).

When you activate your legacy, you aren't just thinking about today, you're stepping into something that will outlive you. You're building something God will multiply beyond what you can see.

ONE STEP OF OBEDIENCE: THE LOVE OUT LOUD STORY

For years, I dreamed of starting Love Out Loud—a way to give back and allow the women in my community to come together to love people out loud. I've always loved to give, and I didn't want to compete with incredible ministries and organizations already doing Kingdom work—I just wanted to be able to pour into them.

But every time I tried to start this nonprofit or create a foundation, I encountered roadblocks. I kept it on my long list of things to do, but it felt impossible.

Then, in November 2021, I hosted one of my *Live Out Loud* events. One of my multimillion-dollar speakers shared how she had become a six-figure giver each year. She was inspiring, but I never expected the phone call that came weeks later.

She called me and said, "I want to donate to your ministry."

I was stunned. I told her I didn't have a ministry but could point her to some of my favorite ones. She responded, "Yes, you do."

The second time she said it, my heart started racing. I knew what she was talking about. She meant Love Out Loud.

I told her my vision, but before I could even finish, she stopped me and said, "I'm making a check out to Love Out Loud for $10,000. You are to get this going by the end of the year."

I was overwhelmed. Excited. Terrified. But I knew this was God.

Then came the roadblocks. The legal steps. The overwhelming process of creating a nonprofit. I almost gave up. There was a woman in need of $10,000, and I told my pastor I was thinking about just handing her the money instead. It would have been easier than pushing through the process.

That's when my pastor asked me a simple but life-changing question, "What were the instructions that came with this seed?"

I paused. The woman who gave me the $10,000 said God told her to give it to my ministry. Not to another person. Not to another cause. To Love Out Loud.

Then he said something I will never forget: "Do not take shortcuts just because you're experiencing roadblocks."

I knew in that moment that this wasn't just about me—it was about finishing what God asked me to build. Legacy is never built on the easy route. It's built in faithfulness.

And then, everything started to unfold in God's perfect timing.

On February 10th, 2022, just days before Valentine's Day, Love Out Loud was officially approved as a nonprofit. That same month, I was scheduled to be a keynote speaker at Hearts for Moms, a nonprofit dedicated to helping single mothers. I had already waived my speaking fee, but I felt the Holy Spirit prompting me to do more.

I had no idea how to fundraise, but I started asking my

community. I thought, *If I could show up with a $5,000 check, that would be incredible.*

Within 24 hours, I had $5,000. Then $12,000. Then $28,000.

At dinner with my best friend, Gilda, we prayed for it to reach $30,000 by the next morning. At midnight, I saw another $1,500 come in.

Then, just a few hours later, I woke up to a message: "I will match whatever your last donation was."

I said, "$1,500," and just like that, we had $30,000.

That morning, as I wrote the hot pink Love Out Loud check, I was in tears.

Then, another miracle happened. A woman from my community called and said she forgot to give online. She was bringing a check.

"$3,000," she said.

I checked my phone and saw that our theme verse for the year was Jeremiah 33:3. By the end of that day, we had raised $33,300—far beyond what I even dreamed of.

Since then, Love Out Loud has continued to grow. That first $10,000 gift turned into $100,000 in our first year. By 2025, we will have given away almost $1,000,000 to ministries around the world.

If I had taken the shortcut, none of this would have happened.

THE LEGACY OF BOLD FAITH & SISTERHOOD

Legacy isn't just about what we build in our lifetime—it's about what continues long after we're gone. Hebrews 11, often called the *Hall of Faith*, reminds us that the greatest heroes of the Bible didn't always see the full reward of their obedience on this side of heaven. Yet, their faith changed the course of history. They moved in obedience, not for immediate gratification, but for a promise that would unfold across generations.

ACTIVATE YOUR IMPACT

"These heroes all died still clinging to their faith, not even receiving all that had been promised them. But they saw beyond the horizon the fulfillment of their promises and gladly embraced it from afar. They all lived their lives on earth as those who belonged to another realm."
(Hebrews 11:13, TPT)

That's the kind of legacy I want to leave for my daughters. I want them—and their children, and their children's children—to *feel* the results of my faith-driven choices, even if I don't see the full reward myself.

Just as the Israelites stepped into the Promised Land because of the faith and obedience of the generation before them, I want my life to be one that sows seeds of impact for generations to come.

When Brett and I considered our legacy, we knew we wanted to live in a way that celebrated every season, shaping a culture of gratitude and joy that would ripple through our family for years.

We decided early on that we wouldn't speak negativity over our daughters' lives. We replaced phrases like *terrible twos* with *terrific twos,* and we refused to buy into the idea that the teenage years had to be hard—we chose instead to call them *exciting teenage years.*

That choice shaped the way we parented. We've intentionally created experiences, traveled, and embraced each stage of their growth, believing that the way we see life directly influences the legacy we leave. We want our daughters to inherit more than just memories—we want them to inherit a mindset of faith, joy, and expectation.

But legacy isn't just about family—it's also about the people we surround ourselves with. One of my constant prayers has been to be surrounded by loving, kind, inspiring, life-giving, and authentic women.

God has answered that prayer in ways beyond what I could have imagined. The work I *get to do* every day has introduced me to an incredible tribe of women—women I lead and mentor, but also women who pour into me. Because let me tell you, leadership can't happen in isolation.

> *"The generous will prosper; those who refresh others will themselves be refreshed."*
> **(Proverbs 11:25, NLT).**

Sisterhood is important. The women we choose to surround ourselves with matter. We need women we can trust, women we can learn from, women who call us higher and breathe life into us when we feel weary.

Just like the faith champions in Hebrews 11 who paved the way for generations after them, there are women in our lives today who remind us to believe bigger, to stand firm in faith, and to step boldly into what God has called us to do.

So, who are those women for you? Who has your front, back, and sides?

Just as importantly, are you *that woman* for someone else? Because legacy isn't just about what you receive; it's about what you *give*. It's about being intentional in how you live, in how you lead, and in how you love. It's about saying *yes* to the hard things now so that generations after you can reap the rewards.

That's the kind of legacy I want to leave. A legacy of faith, boldness, and unwavering trust in God's plan. A legacy that outlives me, strengthens those who come after me, and continues to build His kingdom long after I'm gone.

ACTIVATE YOUR IMPACT

KAT'S STORY

BREAKING CHAINS, BUILDING LEGACY

Let me tell you about one of the most impactful legacies I've seen built so far.

Because legacy isn't just about what you leave behind for your family—it's about the *ripple effect* of who you serve, who you set free, and how God moves through your obedience.

That's exactly what Kat is building. She knew she was called to something more. She knew God had placed a purpose inside of her. But before she could fully step into it, she had to do something radical.

She had to break free.

For nine and a half years, Kat has been sober. But for her, sobriety wasn't just about staying away from alcohol—it was about breaking a generational curse that had gripped her family for decades.

Addiction ran deep in her family, yet no one ever talked about it. No one confronted it. No one called it what it was.

Until Kat.

She was the first to seek help. The first to say, "This stops with me." The first to surrender it all to Jesus.

When she did, something inside of her shifted. Because surrender isn't just about letting go—it's about stepping into freedom.

She always heard people say, "Obedience through Christ brings freedom." But it wasn't until she got sober that she truly understood what that meant. Her entire world opened up.

But here's what I love—her story didn't stop with her personal breakthrough. Kat's transformation accelerated when she surrounded herself with women who called her higher.

When she joined the *Queen's Table*, everything changed. For the first time, she was in a room filled with women who shared her values—women who weren't just talking about purpose, but living it out boldly.

She wasn't just growing in her faith—her faith was *activated*. She found clarity on her purpose. She realized God wasn't just calling her to stay free—He was calling her to *set others free*.

That's when she started taking action.

Kat isn't just rewriting her family's story—she's creating a legacy that will impact generations beyond her own.

One day, when her grandchildren talk about her, she doesn't want them to say she was just strong. She wants them to say she was a *chain breaker,* that she stood in the gap, and that she paved the way for a new legacy—one built on faith, healing, and freedom in Christ.

I've watched her walk this out. When Kat speaks, chains break. She isn't just leading a movement—she is *setting captives free*.

If you've ever doubted whether your story could bring freedom to others, hear me: God will use you if you let Him.

So let me ask you: What legacy are you creating?

Are you holding onto something that needs to be released? Are you staying quiet when God is calling you to *break the chains*?

Because here's what I know: When you step into obedience, you don't just change your life—you change generations.

ACTIVATE YOUR IMPACT

HOW LEGACY IS BUILT

> Legacy starts with obedience. With stewardship. With saying yes to the assignment God has given you. When you operate in obedience, He multiplies what you have. He expands your reach. He deepens your influence.

But here's the challenge: If you *choose* to think and live small, you don't just shrink yourself—you shrink your legacy. You shrink the ripple effect you have on generations to come.

Think about that. If you play small, if you hold back, if you stay silent when you're called to speak, if you refuse to activate what God has placed inside of you—who *misses out* because of that decision?

Your children? Your community? The people you were assigned to impact?

The next generation is watching. They will walk into what you build. They will carry forward what you activate. They will expand what you *choose* to step into.

ACTIVATING YOUR LEGACY

Legacy is activated when you lead boldly. When you take risks in faith. When you refuse to let fear dictate your decisions. When you *do the work* that God has called you to do—even when it's uncomfortable, even when it stretches you, even when the results aren't instant.

The legacy you leave will be determined by the life you *live today*.

So, ask yourself:

- Are you leading in a way that multiplies impact for future generations?
- Are you investing in the people who will carry this forward?
- Are you making decisions with eternity in mind?

Legacy doesn't start when you die. It starts the moment you decide to live differently.

And today, I'm asking you to activate it.

Because you are not just called to build something for yourself—you are called to build something *bigger than you*.

Lead boldly. Live fully. And activate your legacy—starting now.

ACTIVATION 1: INCREASE YOUR INCOME, EXPAND YOUR IMPACT

"But remember the LORD your God, for it is He who gives you the ability to produce wealth, and so confirms His covenant, which He swore to your ancestors, as it is today."
(Deuteronomy 8:18, NIV)

God is not asking you to hustle harder. He's asking you to steward better.

There is provision assigned to your purpose. But provision doesn't always come as a lump sum in your bank account—it comes as an opportunity, an idea, a strategy, a connection. It comes through the wisdom to multiply what's already in your hands.

For too long, Christian women have wrestled with the lie that earning more means they are being selfish. But income is not about accumulation—it's about activation. More income means more opportunities to give, serve, create, and sow into Kingdom work.

If you don't increase your income, you limit your impact.

Provision follows obedience. If you step forward, the resources will follow.

God isn't waiting for the "right time" to bless you. He's waiting for you to step into the increase that already has your name on it.

ACTIVATION 2: WISE WOMEN BUILD LEGACY

"Wise people are builders—they build families, businesses, communities. And through intelligence and insight, their enterprises are established and endure. Because of their skilled leadership, the hearts of people are filled with the treasures of wisdom and the pleasures of spiritual wealth."
(Proverbs 24:3-4, TPT)

A wise woman builds.
She builds her home.
She builds her business.
She builds the next generation.
She builds her legacy.

God is not asking you to maintain what already exists—He is calling you to establish something that will outlive you. What you build today is what the next generation will stand on tomorrow.

Legacy doesn't happen by accident. It is created through intentional leadership, vision, and stewardship. It's the result of showing up daily in excellence, obedience, and unwavering faith.

The world builds for profit. Kingdom women build for purpose.

They build businesses that create impact.

They build families that carry faith.

They build movements that expand the Kingdom.

And here's the truth—what you build will either bless or burden those who come after you.

What are you constructing with your life right now? Are you building with intention, or just going through the motions? A wise woman builds with purpose. And what she builds lasts.

ACTIVATION 3: ASK BIG

"Ask of Me, and I will give You the nations."
(Psalm 2:8, AMPC)

God is not in the business of small prayers. When you come to Him with a request, He's not measuring it against your abilities. He's measuring it against His power.

So why are you still praying small? Do you really believe God is limited?

Because if you did—if you truly believed He is who He says He is—then you wouldn't hesitate to ASK BIG.

Jabez didn't hold back. He boldly asked God to expand his territory—and God said yes.

This is not about material things. This is about believing in the impossible.

The restoration of a broken relationship.

The breakthrough in your business.

The doors that no man can shut.

The salvation of the people you love.

The impact you know you were created for.

What if the only thing standing between you and answered

prayers is the size of your request? Psalm 2:8 doesn't suggest that we ask big—it commands it.

God wants you to step into divine expansion. He is not withholding—He is waiting for you to believe He is capable. The question is: Do you?

SPEAK THIS OUT LOUD:

God, I trust You as my source. I refuse to operate from a place of fear or limitation. I believe that my ability to create income is not just for me—it is for Kingdom impact. I choose to increase my capacity, knowing that as I steward well, You will multiply my efforts. I commit to building with wisdom, creating something that will outlive me. And I refuse to pray small prayers when You have commanded me to ask big.
I will not shrink back. I will expand, increase, and walk in bold faith.
I declare that You are the God of more than enough, and I step into the fullness of what You have prepared for me.

DECLARE THIS OVER YOURSELF:

I DECLARE that I have been given the ability to increase my income and expand my impact.
I DECLARE that I am a builder. I create legacy, opportunity, and Kingdom influence.
I DECLARE that I will not shrink back from financial growth. God has called me to multiply what is in my hands.
I DECLARE that I will pray bold prayers and ask big things, knowing that nothing is impossible for my God.
I DECLARE that I am a faithful steward, a Kingdom investor, and a woman of divine wisdom.

LOL ACTIVATION

Your ability to increase, build, and ask big is already inside of you.

But knowing isn't enough. Activation happens when you take action.

What you believe shapes how you show up.

What you speak determines what you step into.

What you activate determines the legacy you leave behind.

LEARN IT:

Where have you been hesitant to increase your income, expand your impact, or ask boldly? What limiting beliefs have held you back?

ACTIVATE YOUR IMPACT

OWN IT:

What area of your life is God calling you to expand? Where do you need to take action in building legacy, leadership, or financial growth?

LIVE IT:

If you stepped into expansion today without fear or hesitation, what would change? What is one bold action you will take right now to move forward?

Raise your rates.
Launch the thing you've been delaying.
Step into mentorship.
Pray prayers that stretch your faith.

When you move, God moves. And when you ask big, He responds in ways beyond what you can imagine. There is more waiting for you. It's time to activate it.

Chapter Eight

ACTIVATE YOUR PEACE

Peace isn't just a feeling—it's a person. His name is Jesus. And when you activate your peace, you're aligning with Him. You're agreeing to live from a place of rest, no matter what's happening around you.

Peace isn't about pausing everything or stepping away from the work God has called you to. It's about standing firm, knowing you are exactly where He wants you to be, covered, protected, and sustained by His presence.

THE TRUTH ABOUT PEACE

We live in a world that glorifies the hustle—work more, do more, strive for more. But what if I told you that true success doesn't come from the grind, but from resting in God's promises?

The Bible tells us in Matthew 11:28, *"Come to me, all you who are weary and burdened, and I will give you rest."* Jesus didn't say, "Try harder." He said, "Come to me." Peace is found in His presence.

I've met so many high-achieving women who are constantly pouring out, leading their businesses, families, and communities—yet they never stop to ask themselves, *Who is pouring into me?* That's where so many lose their peace. You cannot lead, build, or create from an empty cup. You need to be filled before you can overflow.

THE KEY TO LASTING PEACE

The world will try to convince you that peace comes when everything in your life is in order—when your finances are thriving, your relationships are solid, and your business is booming.

But that's not true peace. The peace Jesus offers is unshakable. It's the kind of peace that remains even when things don't go as planned, when doors close, when unexpected challenges arise.

So, ask yourself: *Is my soul well?* That's the real question. Because if your soul isn't at rest, no external success will ever be enough.

Romans 8:28 reminds us, *"And we know that in all things God works for the good of those who love Him, who have been called according to His purpose."* When you trust that God is working all things for your good, you can let go of the stress, the striving, the fear, and step into peace.

RACHEL'S STORY

ANCHORED IN OBEDIENCE, ACTIVATED IN PEACE

I'll never forget when Rachel walked into one of our *Live Out Loud* events. She carried decades of ministry experience, but also a quiet question in her heart.

"What if God is calling me to something new?"

After 20 years in full-time ministry, Rachel knew how to lead, how to serve, and how to carry the weight of spiritual responsibility. But as the stirring in her heart grew, her peace started to waver.

She told me, "I've spent years supporting my husband's business dreams, but now I feel God nudging me to build something of my own. I just don't know how to bring the business side of my brain into alignment with the ministry side of my heart."

That's the tension many of us feel when standing at the threshold of something unfamiliar. Fear can creep in, convincing us that peace is only found in the familiar, the safe, the known.

But what I saw in Rachel was a woman who was ready to trade comfort for calling, and in doing so, she discovered a deeper peace than she had ever known.

She could have ignored the stirring. She didn't *need* to do anything financially—after all, she had already helped foster over $2 billion in sales through her husband's real estate business.

Since that day, I've watched God completely transform her life. She's been a *Queen's Table* member for several years, boldly building a business that equips others to understand biblical wealth and advance the Kingdom of God. She's creating resources, mentoring leaders, and mobilizing an army of purpose-driven entrepreneurs.

She's not striving. She's not overwhelmed. She's walking in supernatural peace. And here's the most powerful part: She's not doing any of it instead of ministry. She's doing it through ministry. Her business flows from a place of stillness, not striving. She's creating impact without sacrificing her soul.

Rachel's story is proof that peace isn't found in predictability —it's found in obedience. It's the quiet confidence of knowing that God is with you, even when the path ahead is uncertain.

So let me ask you:

What if the very thing that feels unfamiliar or uncomfortable is the invitation to a deeper peace?

What if the peace you've been searching for is found, not in doing more, but in trusting more?

Rachel said yes to that kind of peace. And so can you.

PEACE IN ACTION

Peace doesn't mean passivity. It means confidence. Confidence that God has gone before you. Confidence that you are exactly where He wants you to be. Confidence that no weapon formed against you will prosper (Isaiah 54:17).

But activating peace requires intentionality. Here's how you activate peace in your daily life:

1. **Speak Truth Over Yourself**—The words you declare matter. Every morning, I speak life over myself: *I am a daughter of the Most High. I am filled with the peace of God. No matter what comes against me today, I stand firm in His promises.* When you align your words with God's truth, your soul will follow.
2. **Worship Through the Warfare**—When life feels overwhelming, worship is your weapon. I have seen time and time again that when I pause and lift my hands in worship, my circumstances may not immediately change, but my perspective does. Romans 8:31 reminds us, *"If God is for us, who can be against us?"* Worship shifts your focus from the problem to the promise.
3. **Rest in God's Timing**—Peace means trusting that God's timing is better than yours. Sometimes, you can lose your peace because you're trying to force things to happen when God is saying, *Be still and know that I*

am God (Psalm 46:10). His ways are higher. His plans are greater. And when you release control, you make room for peace.

4. **Let Go of What You Were Never Meant to Carry**—So many of us are carrying burdens that we were never meant to hold. Jesus already paid the price for your worries, your fears, your anxieties. 1 Peter 5:7 says, *"Cast all your anxiety on Him because He cares for you."* If you're feeling heavy, ask yourself: *What do I need to release to God today?*

5. **Surround Yourself With the Right People**—The voices you allow in your life will either stir up peace or steal it. Are the people around you encouraging you, speaking life over you, pointing you back to truth? Or are they filling your mind with doubt, fear, and negativity? Choose wisely.

PEACE IN BUSINESS AND LEADERSHIP

One of the biggest challenges I see in women who lead is that they think rest is a luxury instead of a necessity. But you cannot run a business, lead a team, or fulfill your calling without a foundation of peace.

That's why I created *Lavish*—a retreat for high-achieving women to simply be. No expectations, no pressure, just space to receive. I believe that when you give yourself permission to rest, you activate something powerful. You realign with your purpose. You reconnect with God. You remember why you started in the first place.

I've seen it happen over and over. Women walk into the room carrying so much stress, pressure, and responsibility, and they leave with clarity, peace, and fresh vision. Why? Because they took time to rest in the presence of God.

A FINAL WORD

You were never meant to strive through life. You were created to walk in peace, to live from a place of rest, to operate from overflow. Peace isn't just a nice idea—it's your inheritance.

So today, I challenge you: Activate your peace. Speak truth. Worship boldly. Release control. Trust God's timing. Surround yourself with the right people. Step into what He has for you, and refuse to let anything steal your peace.

Because when you walk in peace, you lead with power. And that changes everything.

ACTIVATION 1: RECEIVE YOUR MIGHTY POWER

"For God will never give you the spirit of fear, but the Holy Spirit who gives you mighty power, love, and self-control."
(2 Timothy 1:7, TPT)

Are you feeling stuck today? Tangled in a web of doubt, worry, or fear? Shake it off and rise up. Fear is not from God. He has promised us the exact opposite—mighty power, love, and self-control.

I keep this verse everywhere—on post-it notes, in my wallet, on my mirror—because this truth transforms me. When I wake up feeling off, face a difficult conversation, or feel resistance in my business, I declare it out loud:

"I receive mighty power over every spirit of fear."

"I claim love instead of rejection, resentment, or unforgiveness."

"I activate self-control that overrides any self-sabotage or weakness."

The Holy Spirit is with you, infusing you with supernatural

strength. You don't have to live in fear—you are armed with power.

Now, I want you to text this verse to a friend. Declare it. Speak it. Share it. Because fearless living is contagious. The more you pass it on, the stronger it becomes.

Choose today to activate peace over panic, power over fear, and strength over weakness. The Holy Spirit is your source—tap into it and watch how your life transforms.

ACTIVATION 2: GOD WORKS ALL THINGS FOR GOOD

> *"And we know that in all things God works for the good of those who love him, who have been called according to his purpose."*
> **(Romans 8:28, NIV)**

Romans 8:28 is my go-to scripture every day. No matter what challenges or struggles arise, I choose to stand on the truth that God *will* work all things out for good.

When you're in the middle of something that feels like a crisis, trauma, or major challenge, this verse can feel like just words. But I promise you—when you look back on the hardest moments of your life, you'll see that God has worked them all out for good.

This is your lifeline when you feel stuck. It is a way to breathe, a way out, a reminder that God will take you up and out. It may not feel like it when you're in the middle of it, but if you do what I'm about to tell you, it will change everything.

Say it once: God will work things together for my good, because He called me according to His purpose.

Say it twice: God will work things together for my good, because He called me according to His purpose.

Say it three times: God will work things together for my good, because He called me according to His purpose.

Let this truth settle into your spirit. God has never failed you, and He will not start now.

Keep speaking it. Keep standing on it. Watch how He turns every struggle, every setback, and every impossible situation into something good.

ACTIVATION 3: REST IN WHO GOD CREATED YOU TO BE

> *"See what great love the Father has lavished on us, that we should be called children of God!"*
> **(1 John 3:1, NIV)**

Rest is not a luxury—it's a command. It's an invitation from God to step into His presence and receive His love without striving.

At my Lavish Retreat, I've seen women walk in heavy—carrying stress, pressure, and expectations—and walk out light, refreshed, and restored. Because something happens when you allow yourself to be seen and known, and simply rest in who God created you to be.

I want you to do something powerful today: Write it down.

What burdens have you been carrying that were never yours to hold?

What stress do you need to release to God?

What would your life look like if you truly trusted Him with your rest?

Write it. Pray over it. Then physically throw it away. Because as long as you hold on to what's weighing you down, you're not fully receiving the rest God has for you.

Jesus said, *"Come to me, all of you who are weary and burdened, and I will give you rest"* (Matthew 11:28, NIV). Let's receive that promise today. It's time to lay it all down and rest.

ACTIVATE YOUR IMPACT

ACTIVATION 4: RECLAIM YOUR PEACE, RELEASE THE PRESSURE

"I am at rest in God alone; my salvation comes from him.
He alone is my rock and my salvation, my stronghold;
I will never be shaken."
(Psalm 62:1-2, TPT)

When did life get so busy? When did we start wearing busyness like a badge of honor?

The enemy wants to keep you distracted, overwhelmed, and overcommitted. Why? Because a rested woman is a dangerous woman.

Priscilla Shirer puts it this way in her book, *FerVent: A Woman's Battle Plan to Serious, Specific, and Strategic Prayer:* "If I were your enemy, I'd make everything seem urgent, as if it's all yours to handle ... If I could keep you busy enough, you'd be too overwhelmed to even realize how much work you're actually saving me."

It's time to reclaim your peace. Right now, take a personal inventory:

What are the pressures and expectations weighing you down?

Where are you feeling exhausted, guilty, or overwhelmed?

What distractions are pulling you away from peace?

Now, declare this truth over yourself:

God alone is my source of peace.

I am at rest in Him—I will not be shaken.

I release pressure, stress, and expectations that were never mine to carry.

Breathe it in. Speak it out. Walk in it. Because peace isn't just a feeling—it's a choice. And today, you choose peace over pressure.

SPEAK THIS OUT LOUD:

God, I trust You as my source of peace. I release every burden, every fear, and every expectation that does not belong to me. I declare that I am covered by Your love and sustained by Your promises.

I refuse to let fear or stress control me. I will not be shaken. I will not be distracted. I will walk in peace, knowing that You are working all things together for my good.

I choose to rest in Your presence, to trust in Your timing, and to release anything that is weighing me down. My peace is not found in my circumstances—it is found in You.

Today, I activate my peace, I stand firm in Your truth, and I declare that I am walking in the fullness of Your rest.

DECLARATIONS: ACTIVATE YOUR PEACE

I DECLARE that fear has no hold on me. God has given me power, love, and a sound mind.
I DECLARE that no matter what I face, God is working all things together for my good.
I DECLARE that I will not carry what was never mine to hold. I release every burden to God and receive His perfect rest.
I DECLARE that I will walk in peace, trusting that God's plan is greater than my own.
I DECLARE that my mind is at rest, my spirit is steady, and my heart is confident in the Lord's promises.
I DECLARE that I am unshaken because my peace is rooted in God alone.

LOL ACTIVATION

Peace isn't something you wait for—it's something you activate.

When you trust that God is working all things together for your good, you release control and step into supernatural rest. This is your moment to realign with Him, let go of the chaos, and walk boldly in His peace.

LEARN IT:

Where have you allowed fear or stress to steal your peace? What have you been holding onto that needs to be surrendered to God?

OWN IT:

What would your life look like if you fully trusted God with your peace? What areas do you need to intentionally let go of?

LIVE IT:

What's one action step you can take right now to reclaim your peace? Will you declare Scripture? Set new boundaries? Release pressure?

Take a deep breath. Peace is already yours. It's time to step into it.

SECTION 3: FAITH

Chapter Nine

ACTIVATE SURRENDER

*S*urrender is the key to unlocking the life God has created for you. It's the step that moves you from striving to thriving, from controlling to trusting, from carrying the weight of everything to releasing it all into His hands.

Too often, we get in our own way. We let doubt, fear, and pride keep us from stepping fully into our calling. We're held hostage by the lies of the enemy:

- *I'm not good enough.*
- *I've been overlooked.*
- *I've been betrayed.*
- *What if I fail?*

These thoughts steal our peace, keep us bound, and stop us from moving forward. But here's the truth: you cannot walk in the fullness of your calling while holding on to disbelief.

So today, I'm asking you the hard questions: *What do you need to surrender? What do you need to lay at the feet of Jesus?*

THE DEPTH OF SURRENDER

For so long, I thought surrender meant giving up. But it's not about giving up—it's about letting go. It's about trusting that God knows what He's doing, even when things don't make sense.

I learned this in one of the hardest seasons of my life—when I faced deep betrayal. My flesh wanted to fight back. I wanted to defend myself, set the record straight, and take control of the situation. But months before this moment, God had been speaking to me about surrender. He had been preparing me for what was coming.

So when it happened, I knew. I knew I had a choice: I could try to control the outcome, or I could surrender and trust that God would fight for me. And that's exactly what He did.

He whispered to my heart, *"Keep moving. I've got this. Don't do anything. Don't talk about it. Speak truth when necessary, but trust Me to take care of the rest."*

That level of surrender? It stretched me. It challenged me. But it also freed me.

I had to surrender my fear, my reputation, and my need to be understood. And in return, God showed me a new level of His faithfulness. He took care of every detail in a way I never could have orchestrated on my own.

There was a moment when I was deep in the study of surrender—really pressing into what it meant to fully trust God with everything.

In the middle of that season, someone sent me a prophecy from Lana Vawser, a well known prophet, author, and teacher. As I read it, I knew it was a word for me. It spoke directly to what I was walking through, confirming so much of what God had been stirring in my heart.

The prophecy said: *"Your depth of surrender to Me is positioning you to stand in new places."*

ACTIVATE YOUR IMPACT

Lana described a deep invitation from the Lord—to *lay down*, *let go*, and *surrender*. She wrote about the pain of releasing things, but how that pain was far outweighed by the love we have for Jesus and the longing to follow His ways.

She described surrender as something that happens in the hidden place, where no one sees, where it's not about proving our devotion, but about offering everything to Him out of pure love. And she said that in that place of quiet surrender, Jesus is moved—moved by our love, our purity of heart, and our faithfulness.

I didn't just read those words—I prayed them over my community. I declared them with expectation because I knew that kind of surrender wasn't just about what I was leaving behind but about what God was preparing me for. And even now, those words continue to bless me.

"Humble yourselves before the Lord, and he will exalt you" (James 4:10, ESV).

> Surrender isn't about loss - it's about positioning. The deeper our surrender, the higher God calls us. When we give Him everything, not for recognition but out of love, He is moved. He sees. And He responds.

GILDA'S STORY

LETTING GO TO STEP IN

I've seen so many women hold onto a career, a title, or a lifestyle that feels safe, even when they know God is calling them to something greater.

I get it. Surrender isn't easy. Letting go of security and stepping into the unknown is terrifying.

That's exactly where Gilda found herself.

For 18 years, she built a career on Wall Street. It was prestigious. It was financially secure. It was the kind of job most people would fight to keep.

But she was miserable.

She spent long hours away from her family doing work that didn't fulfill her. She felt stuck—like she was living a life that looked successful on the outside but felt empty on the inside.

And yet, she stayed. Not because she loved it. Not because she felt called to it. But because walking away didn't seem like an option.

Surrender is hard when comfort is predictable. But God had more.

I've known Gilda for most of my life. She wasn't always walking closely with the Lord, but when she rededicated her life to Jesus at 32, I saw something ignite in her.

God was calling her to something new, but she had to be willing to let go of what she had built.

That's where surrender comes in.

Before she could step into a career of purpose, she had to release the career of comfort. Before she could step fully into her faith, she had to stop relying on her own plan.

But she didn't do it alone. Faith needs activation. And for Gilda, *Live Out Loud* was where her faith came alive.

She didn't just experience a personal shift—she positioned herself in an environment where she saw other women walking in bold faith. Women who had surrendered their own plans and watched God replace them with something better. When she saw that, she started believing for herself.

That's why community matters. When you place yourself in an environment of belief, breakthrough happens faster.

Then, God gave her the next assignment. He told her to leave

Wall Street and buy fitness franchises. A high-level finance executive stepping into full-time entrepreneurship and the fitness industry? It made no sense.

But surrender isn't about logic—it's about trust.

She had no experience in business ownership. She knew nothing about running a gym. But she believed God more than she believed her own abilities.

And that's what surrender looks like.

She didn't need all the answers.

She didn't need a perfect plan.

She just needed to say yes.

And because she did, her entire life changed.

Today, Gilda owns three Burn Boot Camp franchises, is a full-time entrepreneur, and a leader in the marketplace.

But more importantly, she is walking fully in her purpose. Her gyms have become a ministry in the marketplace. They are communities of like-hearted people, cheering each other on, building confidence, and growing stronger—inside and out.

And she knows now—if she hadn't surrendered, she never would have stepped into this calling.

So here's my question for you: What are you still holding onto that God has asked you to release? Is it a career? A title? A plan you created for yourself?

Because here's what I know—what's on the other side of surrender is always greater than what you're afraid to let go of.

God isn't asking you to figure it all out. He's asking you to trust Him.

Let go. Surrender the plan. Step into the unknown.

Because what He has for you is far beyond what you could ever imagine.

TRUE SURRENDER VERSUS FALSE CONTROL

Our human nature fights surrender. We want to control, strategize, and fix things ourselves. But control is an illusion. It exhausts us. It leaves us feeling overwhelmed, burnt out, and fearful.

Surrender is the opposite of striving.

- Striving says, *I have to figure it all out.*
  - Surrender says, *God already has a plan.*
- Striving says, *I need to make this happen.*
  - Surrender says, *God is bringing the increase.*
- Striving says, *I have to protect myself.*
  - Surrender says, *God is my defender.*

When we surrender, we stop trying to do things in our own strength and allow God to take the lead. That's when the pressure comes off. That's when we step into supernatural peace, clarity, and confidence.

THE SUPERNATURAL POWER OF SURRENDER

Every time I've fully surrendered, I've been promoted to a new level. Not by man, but by God.

Jeremiah 17:7-8 (NIV) says: *"Blessed is the one who trusts in the Lord, whose confidence is in him. They will be like a tree planted by the water that sends out its roots by the stream. It does not fear when heat comes; its leaves are always green. It has no worries in a year of drought and never fails to bear fruit."*

Surrender positions you for increase. It removes the burden of self-reliance and allows you to stand firm, knowing that God is in control. It shifts your perspective from fear to faith.

ACTIVATE YOUR IMPACT

THE RESISTANCE TO SURRENDER

Surrender goes against everything our minds have been trained to do. From the time we were young, we were told to work hard, take control of our futures, and make things happen. The world teaches us that control equals power, but according to Jesus, true power is found in surrender.

Our minds will fight it. Our emotions will resist it. But the moment we let go and lean into trust, something shifts.

Think about a child. A child doesn't worry about where their next meal is coming from or if they'll have a place to sleep at night. They simply trust that their parents will provide. That's the kind of trust God wants us to have.

Jesus said in Matthew 18:3 (NIV), *"Truly I tell you, unless you change and become like little children, you will never enter the kingdom of heaven."*

What if we could fully surrender like that? What if we could wake up every morning, lift our hands, and say, *"God, I trust You. I don't know what today holds, but I trust that You do. Lead me."*

HOW TO ACTIVATE SURRENDER IN YOUR LIFE

So how do you surrender in a real, practical way? Here's what it looks like:

1. **Open Your Hands**—Physically open your hands as a sign of releasing control. Pray, "God, I give this to You. I don't want to carry it anymore."
2. **Speak It Out Loud**—Declare what you are surrendering. The enemy works in silence, but freedom comes in speaking truth.
3. **Ask God for His Direction**—Instead of figuring everything out on your own, lean into His wisdom. Jeremiah 33:3 says, *"Call to me and I will answer you*

and tell you great and unsearchable things you do not know."

4. **Worship Through It**—There's power in worship. It shifts your focus from the problem to the promise.
5. **Trust the Timing**—Surrender doesn't mean everything changes instantly. It means trusting God's timing over your own.
6. **Lay Down People-Pleasing**—When we try to please people, we are still holding on to control. True surrender means we care more about what God thinks than what people think.

WHAT ARE YOU STILL HOLDING ON TO?

I want you to pause for a moment. Take a deep breath. What area of your life are you still gripping tightly, trying to control?

Is it your business?

Your finances?

A relationship?

Your health?

Your future?

Make a list. Write down everything you are still carrying—everything you are still striving to fix, manage, or force into place.

Then ask yourself: Am I willing to surrender it today?

Because here's the truth: you cannot receive what God has for you if your hands are full of what you were never meant to carry.

Let's go deeper.

What kind of impact do you want to make? And why is that so important to you?

Now, here's the real question: Are you acting like it? Are you walking, talking, and moving like it's already done—until it is?

ACTIVATE YOUR IMPACT

Or are you stuck? Frozen? Delayed? Maybe you don't think you are—but you are. We all are in some area.

I've worked with tens of thousands of women, and do you know what I've seen over and over again?

There's always something unresolved, something still gripping them.

But by the time we're done here, I want you to name it.

Know what's holding you back.

And release the resistance.

Because you are reading this book on purpose.

Yet maybe right now, you're questioning your purpose. Maybe you're doubting the impact you were made to create.

Because of a diagnosis.

Because of a divorce.

Because of financial challenges.

Because of your circumstances, your situation, your past.

I know exactly how that feels. Twenty-one years ago, a death sentence was spoken over me—stage 3 cancer. Those words took me down a long, dark road to nowhere.

But let me tell you something: no diagnosis, no situation, no person can take away your calling.

I stand here today, two decades later, living proof of what the mercy of God can do. But I had to choose to believe it.

I had to decide to consume a different story.

To speak a different story.

To act on a different story.

To declare, "I will and I am," instead of "I'll try."

Because every word we speak is either life or death.

So, here's the real transition—it's not just about what you're consuming. It's about what you're carrying.

What are you still holding on to?

Things you were never meant to carry.

Words spoken over you.

Betrayal.

Labels from your past.
Shame.
Drama.

I know every single one of you reading this has something. But today, right now, it's time to admit it, let it go, and surrender it.

Because you either carry it, and it entangles you …

Or you release it and walk in freedom, strength, and confidence.

It's time. Toss it. Throw it away. Surrender it all.

And watch what God will do.

FINAL WORD

Surrender isn't weakness. It's power. It's trust. It's walking in the confidence that God has gone before you, that He is making a way, and that His plans are far greater than anything you could orchestrate on your own.

Every single time you activate another level of surrender, you activate another level of breakthrough.

So today, I challenge you: Let go. Open your hands. Surrender your plans, your fears, your need to control. And watch as God moves in ways you never expected.

Because the moment you surrender is the moment you rise up.

ACTIVATE YOUR IMPACT

ACTIVATION 1: THIS SEASON IS FOR A REASON

"I pray with great faith for you, because I'm fully convinced that the One who began this gracious work in you will faithfully continue the process of maturing you until the unveiling of our Lord Jesus Christ."
(Philippians 1:6, TPT)

God never starts something He doesn't intend to finish—including the work He is doing in you.

Did you know that the enemy attacks you hardest at the very place of your highest calling?

Think about where you feel the most resistance, discouragement, and doubt. That is your battleground because the enemy knows your calling. He is trying to keep you from stepping into it. He wants you to think you're too late, too far behind, or too overwhelmed to walk in what God has for you.

But today, I want you to recognize that this season is necessary. It is refining you. Strengthening you. Preparing you.

God is working in you, even when you can't see it.

Even if it feels like you're stuck.

Even if it feels like you should be further along.

Even if it feels like things are not coming together fast enough.

Your today is part of the process for where He is taking you tomorrow. You are in the exact place you need to be for God to complete His work in you. Your calling is not in jeopardy—it is in process.

What if you surrendered to this process instead of fighting against it?

Surrendering to your calling doesn't mean you stop pursuing it. It means you stop striving, controlling, and forcing.

It means you release the anxiety, the doubt, and the pressure to make everything happen in your own strength.

It means you trust that God is the One orchestrating every step.

ACTIVATION 2: SURRENDER TO YOUR WORTHINESS

> *"The blessing of the Lord brings wealth,*
> *without painful toil for it."*
> **(Proverbs 10:22, NIV)**

Have you ever felt unworthy of God's love? Like you need to prove yourself, work harder, or be more to earn His favor?

Have you ever believed you must hustle and grind to receive God's blessings?

I know I have. I've fallen into the mindset that if I just work harder, then maybe I will be worthy of the blessing. But that is not how the Kingdom works.

The world says: If you want more, you have to earn it.

The Kingdom says: If you want more, you have to receive it.

The wealth of the world is tied to striving, stress, and self-reliance. The wealth of the Kingdom is different—it comes from surrender.

God's blessing is not something we hustle for; it is something we align ourselves to receive.

This doesn't mean we don't work hard. It means we don't *toil* in a way that steals our peace, exhausts us, and keeps us from trusting God as our provider.

Have you been trying to force your success? Have you believed that it all depends on you? What would shift if you fully trusted God's provision instead?

Surrendering to your worthiness means you stop striving to earn what God has already promised. It means you stop hustling in fear and start working in faith. It means you trust that what God has for you is greater than anything you could achieve on your own.

ACTIVATION 3: SURRENDER TO TRUST

"Where can I go from your Spirit? Where can I flee from your presence? If I go up to the heavens, you are there; if I make my bed in the depths, you are there. If I rise on the wings of the dawn, if I settle on the far side of the sea, even there your hand will guide me, your right hand will hold me fast."
(Psalm 139:7-10, NIV)

What gets in the way of your trust in God?

Have you been let down, betrayed, or abandoned?

Have you experienced a loss so deep that trusting again feels impossible?

Do you ever feel like your prayers just bounce off the ceiling?

It is easy to let fear creep in when things do not go the way you planned. But here is the truth: God is with you in every season, every storm, and every moment.

Even when you feel abandoned—He is there.

Even when you feel lost—He is leading you.

Even when you feel afraid—He is covering you.

I want to give you a powerful activation to build your trust in Him: The Trust Habit.

Every time fear rises, say this out loud: *"God, I do not like how this feels, but I trust You."*

When you experience loss: *"God, my heart aches, but I trust You."*

When you feel alone: *"God, I feel abandoned, but I trust You."*

When you don't know what to do: *"God, I feel lost, but I trust You."*

When someone betrays you: *"God, I am devastated, but I trust You."*

Faith is activated when trust is spoken.

ACTIVATION 4: SURRENDER TO SUPERNATURAL GROWTH

"But the fruit of the Spirit is love, joy, peace, patience, kindness, goodness, faithfulness, gentleness, and self-control. Against such things there is no law."
(Galatians 5:22-23, NIV)

We have access to the fruit of the Spirit at all times. It is always available, but it is up to us to choose it.

Too often, we let our emotions take over. When things do not go our way, frustration rises. When people disappoint us, impatience sets in. When circumstances feel overwhelming, fear creeps in.

But here is the truth: Your emotions are real, but they are not your leader.

The Holy Spirit allows us to lead with the fruit of the Spirit rather than react out of our emotions. But it requires surrender.

If we rely on our own strength, we will struggle. We will try to force joy when we feel heavy, or force patience when we are at our limit. But we were never meant to manufacture the fruit on our own.

Spiritual growth is not about trying harder—it is about surrendering deeper. We do not produce the fruit of the Spirit by striving. We produce it by staying connected to the Source—by remaining in Him.

Have you ever found yourself in a situation where your first reaction was frustration, anger, or anxiety? In those moments, your natural response may not be patience or peace. But what if you paused and surrendered instead of reacting to your emotions?

What if you stopped and prayed, *"Holy Spirit, show me the fruit I need to choose right now?"*

The fruit is already there—it is just a matter of choosing it.

What fruit do you need to cultivate in this season?

- When you feel impatient, surrender to peace.
- When you feel frustrated, surrender to joy.
- When you feel weary, surrender to His strength.
- When you feel rejected, surrender to His love.
- When you feel rushed, surrender to His patience.
- When you feel overwhelmed, surrender to His self-control.

Choosing the fruit of the Spirit is not about denying your emotions—it is about leading with the Spirit rather than being led by emotions.

When you surrender your emotions to God, something powerful happens: your reactions shift, your perspective changes, and your growth accelerates.

True transformation happens when we let go and allow God to produce the fruit in us.

Are you ready to surrender your emotions and allow the Spirit to lead you?

SPEAK THIS OUT LOUD:

God, I surrender fully. I refuse to live in fear, doubt, or striving. I declare that You are faithful to complete the work You have started in me. I will not shrink back. I release control, knowing that Your plans are higher, Your ways are greater, and Your timing is perfect. I trust You completely.

DECLARE YOUR SURRENDER IS ACTIVATED

I DECLARE I am surrendering every area of my life to God. I will not hold back—I release control and trust His perfect plan!
I DECLARE God is working all things together for my good. Even when I cannot see it, He is moving!
I DECLARE surrender is my strength. I do not have to carry the weight—God is my source, my provider, and my defender!

LOL ACTIVATION

Surrender is not a one-time decision—it is a daily activation.

LEARN IT:

Where are you still holding on instead of surrendering? What area of your life have you struggled to release to God?

OWN IT:

What fear has been keeping you from fully trusting God's process? What would change if you surrendered it today?

LIVE IT:

If you chose full surrender today—without hesitation—what would change in your life, business, and faith? What is one action step you will take right now to activate surrender?

Chapter Ten

ACTIVATE YOUR BELIEF

What if I told you that everything you're waiting for—every breakthrough, every opportunity, every next-level moment—is waiting on *you* to believe?

Belief changes everything. It shifts atmospheres, fuels momentum, and unlocks doors you never thought possible. The level at which you believe will determine what you see unfold in your life.

So, I have to ask—what are you believing for? Are you believing small, or are you believing at the highest level?

I talk about belief all the time because I know that it is the single most important factor in stepping into everything God has called you to do. Yet, so many people let doubt, discouragement, or distractions water down their belief. If you want to activate your impact, you must activate your belief.

THE POWER OF AN ATMOSPHERE OF BELIEF

Have you thought about your atmosphere lately? Who are you hanging around? It matters! The level of belief in the people around you *matters*.

Have you ever noticed how successful people position themselves in environments where they are constantly challenged to grow? They seek out spaces where others believe bigger, think bigger, and *expect* more.

When I get into a space where belief is the standard, my confidence grows, my capacity expands, and my faith is strengthened.

That's why I love to *announce and honor* the success of others in all of my businesses and communities. Some people shy away from celebrating success, but I do the opposite—I *showcase* it.

Why? Because belief grows when we see what's possible. I want people to shine so others can look and say, "*God, if You can do it for her, You can do it for me!*" Never from a place of jealousy, but from a spirit of belief. When we celebrate what God is doing in others, we activate belief in our own lives. This is what we should be teaching the next generation!

NOEMI'S STORY

BELIEF CHANGES EVERYTHING

When I first met Noemi, I could see she was a powerhouse. A brilliant attorney, a leader, and a mother—she carried strength, confidence, and success. But I also sensed something deeper.

Underneath it all, she was searching. Searching for a way to fully integrate her faith into her business, to lead boldly with biblical principles, and to step into an unshakable purpose.

ACTIVATE YOUR IMPACT

What I didn't realize was just how much God had planned to activate in her all along.

As Noemi stepped into this community, she didn't just learn strategies—she had a personal encounter with Jesus. She started getting serious about the Word, digging into scripture, and allowing God to reshape the way she showed up in every area of her life.

The transformation was undeniable. She went from feeling like she didn't belong to realizing that she was exactly where God had called her to be. She saw that this wasn't just about business—it was about her purpose. Once that clicked, everything changed.

Noemi's law firm became more than a business—it became a Kingdom assignment. She started leading Bible studies in her office, praying over cases, and creating a space where God's presence is welcome in an industry that desperately needs light. She became the kind of leader who doesn't waver, who stands firm on biblical principles, and who makes decisions rooted in faith.

Here's the thing—this wasn't just about business growth (though that happened too). It was about transformation from the inside out. Before God could take Noemi's business to a new level, He had to strengthen the foundation—her identity, her confidence in Him, and her ability to steward both her calling and her finances with wisdom.

If you ask Noemi what the biggest shift in her life has been, she won't tell you about numbers or revenue. She'll tell you that she has fallen in love with Jesus on a deeper level than she ever imagined.

That is the ultimate success. At the end of the day, when we *Live Out Loud* for Jesus, when we build businesses that glorify Him, when we align every part of our lives with His Word—**our purpose becomes activated.**

KEEP YOUR BLINDERS ON

You should never debate your dreams with someone else. They are *your* dreams. God placed them inside of *you* for a reason. Everyone is uniquely created to walk out their own calling, and when you understand that, comparison loses its power over you. You can be inspired by what God is doing in the lives of others while knowing He has something uniquely designed for you.

The enemy wants you distracted. He wants you caught up in comparison, questioning your path, second-guessing what God already told you.

Comparison will keep you stuck. It will make you doubt what is already *yours* in the Kingdom of God. That's why you have to put on your blinders. Don't look to the left or the right. Keep your focus on what God has called *you* to.

That's also why I believe in cultivating a *culture of celebration.* When we celebrate others, it fuels our faith. It reminds us that God is moving, that breakthrough is happening, and that He is faithful. Be encouraged by what others are doing, let it strengthen your belief, and keep pursuing what God has placed in your heart.

FAITH MOVES MOUNTAINS

Mark 9:23 says, *"Everything is possible for one who believes."* Do you actually believe that? Because if you did, you would move differently. You would take action with confidence. You would speak differently. You would expect miracles.

I have always been an *all in* kind of person. When I commit to something, I don't waver. I don't entertain backup plans. I don't step in halfway. I go all in. Why? Because I know that belief requires full commitment. You can't just dip a toe into your calling and expect to see full results. You have to decide—*I'm all in, no matter what.*

That's where faith comes in. You have to believe so fully in what God has called you to do that quitting is not an option. You have to believe so strongly that no delay, no setback, no challenge can shake your confidence. Because here's the truth: *nobody and nothing can stop your calling unless you fall out of belief.*

The enemy will try. He will throw distractions, doubt, and discouragement your way. But the only way he wins is if you agree with him. If you let unbelief take root, you step out of alignment with what God is doing. But when you stay in belief—when you stay *all in*—nothing can stop what God has already set in motion.

MORGAN'S STORY

LEADING WITH BELIEF, BUILDING WITH FAITH

In 2012, Morgan Kline took a leap that most people wouldn't dare to take.

At only 24 years old, she left a stable corporate job at Kellogg's—a career with security, predictability, and a clear path forward—to start a fitness business with nothing but a vision. No roadmap. No guarantees. Just belief.

Alongside her husband, she launched Burn Boot Camp—from a parking lot. They had no physical location. No proven model. Just an unwavering commitment to their mission: to help transform lives through fitness.

And that belief was tested. There were moments when doubt crept in. There were challenges that threatened to stop her in her tracks. There were seasons where the weight of leadership felt heavier than she ever imagined.

But Morgan didn't waver. She kept believing in the vision.

She kept believing in the people around her. Most importantly, she kept believing that God had called her to this for a purpose far greater than she could see.

Here's what I love most about Morgan—she has never believed that faith should be walked alone. She knows that who you surround yourself with matters.

In 2017, she felt God leading her to seek out a new level of community—a space where she could elevate her faith, share stories of perseverance, and be surrounded by women who were passionate about both their purpose and their families. That's when she stepped into the *Queen's Table* and the *Live Out Loud* community.

It was a game changer.

Morgan and I have known each other for over 13 years, and I've had the honor of watching her journey unfold. She has always carried strength, resilience, and deep belief. But in this season, I saw her step into an even greater level of clarity, faith, and confidence.

She realized that faith is strengthened in community. She surrounded herself with women who elevated her, challenged her to grow, and kept her grounded in truth. And that changed everything.

Morgan has always led with belief—but now, she leads with an even deeper level of conviction and faith.

After ten years of franchising their business, she became the CEO of a company that has generated over a billion dollars in the marketplace, and she does it while being an intentional, faith-filled wife and mother. She has redefined what it means to be a bold, faith-driven CEO who doesn't separate success and obedience but sees them as fully connected.

One of the greatest honors of my work is mentoring women like Morgan—women who are already leaders but are ready for deeper alignment with God's vision for their lives.

ACTIVATE YOUR IMPACT

Because belief alone doesn't activate purpose, faith in action does.

Morgan is living proof that when you build with faith, lead with conviction, and surround yourself with the right people, you unlock a level of strength and impact that you simply cannot find alone.

PRAYING BOLDLY & SPEAKING LIFE

I used to think bold prayers were for pastors or people with deep theological training. But then I realized that bold prayers are for *anyone* who believes. When you pray boldly, you activate belief. You step into agreement with God's promises. You speak life over your situation.

So if you're in a season where your belief feels shaky, start praying out loud. Declare God's Word over your life. Speak life over your business, your health, your family, your dreams. And when doubt tries to creep in, say it out loud: *I believe, I believe, I believe.*

> *The more you speak belief, the stronger it gets. The stronger it gets, the more unstoppable you become.*

HOW TO REMAIN IN A SPIRIT OF BELIEF

True belief must be as strong as steel—so strong that it doesn't bend on a bad day. Hard days will come. Emotional days will come. But the difference between someone who wavers and someone who walks in bold faith? Recovery time. The faster you recover, the faster you move forward.

So much of my expansion of faith and belief came from the

book *The Good Fight of Faith* by Alan Vincent. I've read this book cover to cover three times, and it has deeply influenced and elevated my understanding of belief. It's filled with truths that align with what I share in this chapter.

Mark 9:24 says, *"I believe; help my unbelief."* This is where belief starts—with honesty before God. Admit where you have doubt, and then declare out loud that you believe. Speak it so the enemy hears you. Speak it because your belief level determines what moves in your life.

Belief isn't passive. It's active. It requires responsibility. You cannot ride on someone else's faith forever. I can create an atmosphere of belief, but at some point, you must build it for yourself. Faith comes from hearing the Word of God (Romans 10:17), so immerse yourself in it. Read scripture. Declare it. Sing it. Pray it.

Here are the tools I use to remain in belief:

- **Prayer**—Aligning my words and thoughts with God's truth.
- **Worship**—Shifting my focus back to Him.
- **Trusted friends**—People who remind me who I am in Christ.
- **Journals & notes**—Written records of what God has spoken.
- **The armor of God**—Standing firm against doubt and fear.
- **The fruits of the Spirit**—Living in love, joy, peace, and patience.

God cannot meet us at unbelief. Alan Vincent says, "God is such a righteous God ... He can't meet us at unbelief. He doesn't control us."

Instead, He calls us to rise—to step into belief. Until we choose faith, we remain stuck. Transformation starts with us.

ACTIVATE YOUR IMPACT

Unbelief cripples. The disciples struggled with it even when Jesus stood in front of them. The devil plants doubt because he knows belief is the key to Kingdom advancement. But Jesus rebuked unbelief and called His disciples higher.

We must do the same. Admit where doubt exists, repent, and step into faith. Our belief is what moves mountains, shifts atmospheres, and unlocks the next level of impact.

ACTIVATE YOUR BELIEF NOW

Right now, I want you to take inventory. What are you believing for? Where have you allowed doubt to creep in? What lies have you entertained that need to be replaced with truth?

Write down everything you've been doubting. Cross it out. Then write the opposite—what you WILL do, what you CAN do, what you ARE stepping into.

Belief requires you to decide right now that you will believe at the highest level. That you will step into everything God has for you. That you will take action. That you will *activate your belief* and never look back.

This is your moment. Step into it. Believe at the highest level. And watch what God does next.

ACTIVATION 1: GET YOUR HOPES UP

"'For I know the plans I have for you,' declares the LORD, 'plans to prosper you and not to harm you, plans to give you hope and a future.'"
(Jeremiah 29:11, NIV)

Do you remember what it felt like to have childlike faith? Back when dreaming was effortless, and believing was second nature? Before the world told you to "be realistic" or to "guard your heart" against disappointment?

Somewhere along the way, we stopped letting ourselves get excited. We started lowering expectations, bracing for impact, and making peace with "just in case." But that is not how God designed you to live. Getting your hopes up is not reckless—it is faith.

Jesus said in Matthew 18:3, *"Unless you change and become like little children, you will never enter the kingdom of heaven."*

That means childlike hope isn't just a nice idea, it's how the kingdom of God operates. God delights when you believe boldly. He never tells you to quiet your dreams. He never asks you to make peace with disappointment. He calls you to live with expectation.

Jeremiah 29:11 is one of the most powerful promises in the Bible. When you speak it over your life, something shifts. I have seen this verse break chains off women in an instant. Rescued from anxiety, unbound from depression, elevated from despair, unchained from unforgiveness—just by speaking this promise out loud.

There is unstoppable power in the promises of God. No situation is beyond His touch. No emotions are too heavy for Him to lift. No doubt can cut you off from His goodness. No sickness is stronger than His power to heal. No financial challenge is greater than His ability to provide.

If you feel hopeless or defeated in any area, say Jeremiah 29:11 out loud. Declare His good plans over your life. Say it again and again until you believe it is true.

ACTIVATION 2: BELIEVE BIGGER

"Never doubt God's mighty power to work in you and accomplish all this. He will achieve infinitely more than

ACTIVATE YOUR IMPACT

your greatest request, your most unbelievable dream, and exceed your wildest imagination."
(Ephesians 3:20, TPT)

What would it look like to believe for infinitely more than your greatest request?

Really think about that. What would happen if you truly believed God would do more than you can even dream up?

Ephesians 3:20 is a reminder that God sees everything so much bigger than we do. His wisdom, His resources, and His ability to provide are greater than our wildest imagination. His calling always comes with equipping.

So many people shrink their dreams to fit their current circumstances. They pray for just enough. They adjust their expectations to match what seems reasonable. But God is not in the business of just enough. He is a God of more than enough.

Write down your biggest dreams—the ones that seem wild and unattainable. The ones that make you a little scared to say out loud. These are God-sized dreams. Write down dreams for your family, your business, your health, your home, your future. Any area of your life where you need more.

When you put your faith in God's power, you are stepping into His supernatural ability to do more than you can ask or imagine. Breathe life into your dreams by writing them out and declaring God's power to exceed them.

ACTIVATION 3: BLESS ME A LOT

"And Jabez called on the God of Israel saying, 'Oh, that You would bless me indeed.'"
(1 Chronicles 4:10, NKJV)

Jabez did not whisper a cautious prayer. He did not hold back. He asked boldly. And do you know how God responded? He said yes.

In the Bible, when someone said "indeed," it meant a lot.
Underline.
Bold.
Italics.
Exclamation points.
All caps.
A lot.

Jabez cried out for an abundant blessing, and God gave it to him.

Somewhere along the way, many of us started thinking we had to be careful with our prayers. That asking God for more was selfish. That we should be content with what we have. But when we ask God for more, we are not just asking for our benefit; we are asking so we can be a greater blessing to others.

God wants to expand your influence. He wants to increase your capacity. He wants to multiply what is in your hands so that you can impact more people for His kingdom.

So today, ask Him boldly. Pray the prayer of Jabez: *"Lord, bless me and bless me a lot. Bless my family, my health, my relationships, my business, my finances. Multiply my territory and multiply my influence. Stay with me, protect me, and do everything with me and through me."*

Pay special attention to that last one. We are not supposed to do life on our own. The Lord wants us to think of the impossible and ask Him to do it with us. That is the whole point. We serve a God who makes the impossible possible every single day.

Now, it is your turn. Ask boldly. Believe for more. Declare His blessing over your life.

ACTIVATE YOUR IMPACT

SPEAK THIS OUT LOUD:

God, I believe in Your promises. I refuse to let doubt, distraction, or discouragement water down my faith. I declare that I am a person of bold belief—fully committed, unwavering, and expectant for all that You have for me. My belief activates my breakthrough, fuels my momentum, and unlocks doors I never thought possible. I choose to see my life, my business, and my calling through the lens of faith, knowing that You are the God of more than enough. I will not shrink my prayers or lower my expectations—I will believe bigger, dream boldly, and trust that You are working in ways beyond what I can see. My belief is not passive; it is active. I take full responsibility for my faith, and I choose to stand firm, knowing that what You have spoken over my life will come to pass!

DECLARE YOUR BELIEF IS ACTIVATED

I DECLARE I am a person of unwavering belief. My faith is strong, my confidence is unshakable, and I stand firm in God's promises!

I DECLARE my belief fuels my momentum. I will not hesitate or second-guess what God has already spoken over my life!

I DECLARE I will believe at the highest level. I will not settle for small thinking or limited expectations—I will step into God's Ephesians 3:20 promises!

I DECLARE doubt and fear have no place in my life. I refuse to entertain thoughts of unbelief—I choose faith over fear every single time!

I DECLARE I will steward my belief well. I will align my words, my actions, and my atmosphere with the truth of God's Word, knowing that my belief is the key to unlocking everything He has for me!

LOL ACTIVATION

Belief is the key that unlocks your next level. Everything you're waiting for—every breakthrough, every opportunity, every miracle—is waiting on you to believe.

Your belief determines what you step into.

What you step into determines what you steward.

And what you steward determines how God expands you next.

If you want to see the impossible happen, you must believe it's possible. No hesitation. No half-hearted prayers. No shrinking back. It's time to go all in on belief.

So let's do this. With bold faith, relentless expectation, and a commitment to activate belief in every area of your life, answer the following questions:

LEARN IT:

Where have you allowed doubt to take root? Where have you been holding back in your belief?

ACTIVATE YOUR IMPACT

OWN IT:

What is one area in your life where God is calling you to believe bigger? Where have you been praying small when God is asking you to pray boldly?

LIVE IT:

If you fully activated your belief today—without hesitation, without doubt—what would change? What is one step you will take right now to align your actions with your faith?

Now, take a deep breath and declare: *I believe, I believe, I believe.* Because when you activate your belief, you activate your impact.

Chapter Eleven

ACTIVATE YOUR OBEDIENCE

Obedience is where faith gets real. It's easy to trust God when things feel safe, predictable, and comfortable. But real obedience? That's when you step out, even when it doesn't make sense. That's when you surrender your plan for His. That's when you activate a level of faith that moves mountains.

Matthew 22:37 says, *"Love the Lord your God with all your heart and with all your soul and with all your mind."* Loving God isn't just about words—it's about action. Obedience is proof of our love, proof of our trust, and proof that we believe His way is better than ours.

I've learned that obedience isn't passive—it's an active, intentional choice. It requires faith. It requires trust. And most of all, it requires surrender. I had to surrender my plans, my comfort, and my timing—because on the other side of obedience is fruit, favor, and breakthrough. But getting there? That's where the battle happens.

Who is on the other side of your obedience?

When we make our lives about ourselves—our comfort, our

preferences, our timelines—we limit the breakthroughs God wants to bring. But when we surrender and say, *God, whatever You want, I'm in,* we step into something greater. We step into divine alignment.

Every breakthrough I've ever had has come after a season of breaking, shaking, and rearranging. It's uncomfortable. It's stretching. But it's always worth it. Because the other side of obedience is blessing. It's impact. It's legacy.

A PRAYER THAT CHANGES EVERYTHING

There's a prayer I pray often. It's simple, yet it holds the power to activate my obedience like nothing else. It's not about asking for success, growth, or favor. Instead, it's a bold declaration of faith—thanking God for what He is already doing. Thanking Him for the desires He has placed in my heart and trusting that He is moving, even before I see it.

But I call it my **"scary prayer"** for a reason. The first part of the prayer fills me with confidence:

"Lord, thank You for what You are already doing. Thank You for the dreams You've placed in my heart, for the prayers I've lifted up, and for the plans You are unfolding. I trust that You are already at work."

That part feels safe. It strengthens my faith and reminds me that God is moving.

But the second part? That's where obedience is activated.

"And Lord, if I have this wrong—if this is not from You—take it away. And take it away fast."

That's the hard part. That's the part that requires complete surrender. Because when I say it, I am giving God permission to strip away anything that isn't aligned with His will. I am releasing control.

"Lord, remove everything that is not from You."

The moment those words leave my mouth, I feel the weight

of what I've just prayed. I'm not just asking for clarity or blessings, I'm giving God full authority to redirect me, even if it means taking away something I deeply desire.

And He does.

Because obedience isn't just about moving forward when God says "go." It's also about being willing to stop, shift, or let go when He says "no."

When I first prayed this prayer, everything shifted. Doors I thought were meant for me closed. Relationships changed. Plans I had built in my own strength crumbled.

At first, it felt like a loss. But in reality, it was the greatest realignment of my life.

That prayer was both my breaking point and my breakthrough. It positioned me for the real calling God had for me.

And let me tell you—when you ask God to make room for His best, He will. But you have to be willing to let go.

So let me ask you: What are you holding onto that might not be from God?

If you're serious about walking in purpose, I challenge you to pray that same prayer. It won't be easy, but I promise it will be worth it.

WHEN THE PROPHECY FELT TOO BIG

In 2020, Brett and I went to a revival and did a three-day water fast. I wanted to hear from God in a new way. I'll never forget when a pastor walked up to me and prophesied over my life. He spoke about me becoming a spiritual mother to women, about my business going global, about a calling far bigger than I had ever imagined.

At the time, it felt overwhelming. It felt too big. But here's the thing about obedience: It calls you into places you're not fully ready for.

Four years later, I've watched that prophecy come to life.

Women at my retreats—women older than me—have told me, "You're like a spiritual mother to me." My business has gone global. And none of it happened overnight. It happened through consistent obedience—taking steps forward even when I couldn't see the full picture.

The more I obey, the more I trust. The more I trust, the more I see God move. And the more I see God move, the more I realize obedience always leads to fruit.

THE PRESSURE IS OFF WHEN YOU SERVE AN AUDIENCE OF ONE

One of the greatest lessons I've learned is this: I'm not here to serve people before I serve God.

When we live to please people, the pressure is exhausting. We're constantly worrying—*What do they think? Am I good enough? Will this work?* But when we shift our focus and serve an audience of One, everything changes. The pressure lifts. We realize that God has already called us, already qualified us, and already made a way for us.

If I'm consumed with what people think of me, I'm not thinking about the people I'm called to serve. That's why I always ask myself: *Who is on the other side of my obedience?* When I stop making it about me and start making it about the Kingdom of God, breakthrough happens.

JEN'S STORY

SAYING YES TO THE "AND"

From my first conversation with Jen Jones, I could feel her conviction. She was a woman who knew how to hear from God and move in obedience. She had already made bold, faith-filled decisions in her life and business, but I could also sense that she was looking for something more.

When I got on my first call with Jen, something clicked. It wasn't just a business opportunity for her. It wasn't just about strategy or growth. This was an assignment. She knew without hesitation that stepping into the *Live Out Loud* community was her next step of obedience. And I knew God was about to expand her leadership in a way she hadn't even imagined.

Jen had always been multi-passionate, balancing business, motherhood, and ministry. She had never believed the lie that you have to choose between success and faith, or between career and family.

But for years, she felt like she was navigating that belief alone. The world kept saying, *Pick one.* But she knew deep in her spirit: *God called me to all of this.*

When she stepped into this community, that belief was confirmed. I watched Jen step fully into the woman God had created her to be. She stopped questioning how it all fit together and started integrating every part of her calling. She realized that obedience to God doesn't require an either/or choice—it activates the "AND."

She didn't have to choose between being a present mom, a minister, and a successful businesswoman—she could be all three. That wasn't wishful thinking; it was divine strategy.

When she stopped wondering if she was giving up too much or being unfaithful to God's call and instead embraced her unique path, she soared. Her confidence grew. Her vision expanded. Her faith deepened. And as she walked in total obedience, she unlocked a new level of impact, influence, and success.

I love that Jen didn't just apply this revelation to her own life; she started sharing it. She began to show other women what was possible when they stopped believing the lie that obedience means limitation. She became a voice for women who are called to more, women who feel pulled in multiple directions, and women who are ready to say YES to the "AND."

Because here's the truth: God is not asking you to choose between your callings. He's calling you to trust that He has designed them to work together.

You don't have to fit into the world's expectations. You don't have to explain or justify what God is calling you to. You just have to be obedient.

Jen's story is proof that when you say yes to God's plan, He will show you how it all fits together—and how it's even bigger than you imagined.

OBEDIENCE LOOKS LIKE ACTION

I've had to learn to let go of my need to control everything. I love to plan, to be organized, and to know exactly how things will unfold. But obedience requires faith in the unknown. It requires responding to the Holy Spirit in real-time.

There have been moments—on stage, in retreats, in conversations—when I've felt God telling me to shift, say something unplanned, and let go of my notes. And when I obey? **That's when the miracles happen.**

God speaks to all of us in different ways. It might be a gut feeling. A whisper in your spirit. A knowing deep inside. When that happens, don't ignore it. Don't rationalize it away. **Move. Speak. Act.**

FEAR IS A TRAP–FAITH IS THE KEY

Let me be real with you: Fear isolates. Fear discourages. Fear delays. And one of the biggest tactics of the enemy is to use discouragement to keep you from stepping into your calling.

But when we activate obedience—when we move forward despite fear—we step into something powerful.

ACTIVATE YOUR IMPACT

That's why it's so important to protect the voices we let into our lives. I started imagining everyone around me saying, *You go, girl!* It might sound silly, but that mindset shifted everything. I surrounded myself with people who lifted me higher. And that's exactly what we do in this community—we rise by lifting others.

So let me remind you: Do not debate your dreams. God gave them to you for a reason.

How often do we second-guess what God has placed on our hearts? We analyze, we overthink, we delay. But here's the truth: If God put it in you, He intends for you to walk it out. The dreams in your spirit aren't random. They're divine assignments. Delaying them because of fear or doubt doesn't make them go away—it just postpones the impact you're meant to have.

Why not you? Why not now?

If you're waiting for a perfect moment, let me tell you—it doesn't exist. Obedience isn't about waiting until you feel ready. It's about stepping out in faith even when you aren't.

People are waiting on the other side of your obedience. There are lives that will be changed, legacies that will be built, and breakthroughs that will happen—not because of anything you can do in your own strength, but because of what God wants to do *through* you.

Take the next step even if it's messy or imperfect. Trust that God will meet you there. He always does.

I'm cheering you on every step of the way.

MELISSA'S STORY

OBEDIENCE OVER COMFORT

I'll never forget watching Melissa's journey unfold. From the moment she joined the *Live Out Loud Elite Mastermind*, I could tell she was a woman who walked in deep faith—one who didn't just talk about obedience, but truly lived it out.

Melissa and her husband, Jonathan, had been praying the same prayer for years:

"Lord, send us. Use us however You want. We will go where You lead, say what You want us to say, and do what You ask us to do."

And let me tell you—when you pray a prayer like that, God will answer.

For Melissa and her family, obedience wasn't just about saying yes to what made sense. It meant saying yes to hard things—things that, by the world's standards, seemed irrational, uncomfortable, and even impossible.

When she first considered joining, it didn't seem logical. They had a successful business, but at the time, investing in this community wasn't something they had planned for. Yet, when she prayed, she knew God was leading her here. So she said yes.

That yes changed everything.

Over the next four years, I watched Melissa grow—not just in business, but in every part of her life. Her mindset expanded, her faith deepened, her relationships strengthened, and her vision multiplied. But here's what I love most: through every challenge, every transition, every act of obedience, she never let go of her trust in God.

And God kept stretching her.

At one point, He asked their family to sell everything and move to a new city three hours away from their friends, their community, and the life they had built. It didn't make sense. It wasn't what they had planned. But they obeyed.

Then, He told them to put their boys in school after homeschooling them for years. Again, it didn't make sense. But they obeyed.

Every decision felt uncomfortable. Every step required faith. But through it all, Melissa kept listening. She kept trusting. She kept choosing surrender over certainty.

And what happened?

Because of those acts of obedience, Melissa and her husband are now running a Kingdom-minded investment fund, stewarding and multiplying wealth not just for their family, but for other believers. They have seen God expand their influence, their impact, and their ability to serve others in ways they never imagined.

Melissa will tell you that every single "yes" they've given to God—every hard, painful, uncomfortable step—has led to a blessing they never saw coming. Their marriage is thriving. Their family is stronger than ever. Their faith has deepened. And their trust in God has become unshakable.

She has learned that when you say yes to God, He will always lead you somewhere better than you could have planned for yourself.

If you take one thing from Melissa's story, let it be this: Sometimes obedience won't make sense in the moment, but trust that God sees what's ahead.

He is good. He is faithful. He never leaves us. And when we surrender to His leading, we walk straight into the life we were created for.

ACTIVATION 1: FIND YOUR EDGE

"Have I not commanded you? Be strong and courageous. Do not be afraid; do not be discouraged, for the LORD your God will be with you wherever you go."
(Joshua 1:9, NIV)

God wasn't making a suggestion to Joshua. He wasn't offering a soft encouragement. He gave a command: Joshua, be strong! Be courageous! Don't be afraid! Keep your chin up! No matter how far into enemy territory you advance, the Lord your God will be with you!

Now think about this. Joshua was about to lead the Israelites into the Promised Land, but it wasn't empty. There were 31 kings standing in their way. That's a lot of battles against powerful enemies.

But here's the thing—God gave Joshua a unique strategy for every single one of them.

In one battle, He told Joshua to march around the city walls until they collapsed. Another time, He had him trap five kings in a cave before defeating them. Israel's mission was too big to recycle the same game plan over and over. Joshua had to stay close to God and listen for His voice every single day.

The same is true for us. God calls us to be strong and courageous, but He also promises to guide us every step of the way. He does not ask you to figure it all out on your own. The key to winning your battles is staying connected to His voice.

You aren't limited to the resources you have—heaven's storehouses are packed with everything you need. You don't have to rely on your own understanding—God will give you wisdom when it counts. When you step outside the known and fly past your comfort zone, you become the healer, the world-changer, the difference-maker that God created you to be.

ACTIVATE YOUR IMPACT

God will give you an edge in every battle. Don't be afraid to take on those 31 kings in your life or business. Stay tuned into His voice. Keep your eyes forward. Move in obedience. Strength and courage are your portion.

ACTIVATION 2: SPEAK LIFE

"The tongue has the power of life and death, and those who love it will eat its fruit."
(Proverbs 18:21, NIV)

Have you ever had a single compliment shift the course of your day? It could have been as simple as someone loving your shoes, or as deep as someone calling out your greatness. The words we speak have that same power—not just for others, but for ourselves.

The words you release into the world are like seeds. Will your words grow weeds or flowers?

Proverbs 18:21 makes it clear: words are not neutral. They either bring life or they bring death. They either build or they destroy. They either heal or they wound.

Every word that comes out of your mouth is a choice. If you choose wisely, the ripple effect can be astonishing. Encouragement is free, so give it freely!

Speak life over your family. Speak life over your business. Speak life over your body, your finances, your dreams, your future.

Affirm those around you. Let people know they are valuable, they are important, they matter. Choose to be a person who waters others with words of truth, love, and encouragement.

ACTIVATION 3: YOU GET WHAT YOU GIVE

"A generous person will prosper;
whoever refreshes others will be refreshed."
(Proverbs 11:25, NIV)

"It's better to give than to receive." How many times have we heard that? But did you know Jesus originally said it? It's not just a nice saying—it's a divine principle.

There's an undeniable truth tucked inside generosity: you get what you give.

We live in a world that pushes a "me first" mentality. That's why real generosity catches people off guard. It's refreshing. It stands out. And it carries power.

Remember the widow at Zarephath in 1 Kings 17? There was a famine in the land. She had just enough flour and oil left to make one final meal for herself and her son before they starved. But when the prophet Elijah asked her for a meal, she gave it to him. She chose generosity in a moment of lack.

And what happened? Her flour and oil never ran out. She gave, and she was sustained.

This is how God's kingdom works. When you refresh others, you will be refreshed. When you give, you will receive. When you serve, you will be blessed.

The world needs your generosity more than ever. Pay for someone's dinner. Offer a listening ear. Give your time without expecting anything in return.

Do not be afraid of giving too much, serving too much, or pouring out too much. You will never outgive God. When you live with open hands, He will always fill them.

ACTIVATE YOUR IMPACT

ACTIVATION 4: NO JUDGMENT HERE

"So stop being critical and condemning of other believers, but instead determine to never deliberately cause a brother or sister to stumble and fall because of your actions."
(Romans 14:13, TPT)

Imagine standing in an angry crowd, stones in hand, ready to condemn a woman caught in sin. You can feel the heat of judgment in the air. But then Jesus steps in, bends down, and writes in the sand.

And then He says, *"Let the one who has never sinned throw the first stone."*

Silence.

One by one, the stones drop.

And when the dust settles, Jesus looks at the woman and asks, *"Where are your accusers? Didn't even one of them condemn you?"*

"No, Lord," she says.

And Jesus responds, *"Neither do I. Go and sin no more."*

That moment changed everything.

Romans 14:13 offers us the same opportunity—a chance to drop our stones. To walk away from judgment and step into love.

Paul tells us to stop being critical and condemning, not just of others, but of ourselves. This is freeing. It means we do not have to tear others down, and we do not have to tear ourselves down either.

But do not miss the second half of the verse. Paul also tells us not to "deliberately cause a brother or sister to stumble."

This is not just a caution—it is a call to help others rise.

Jesus did not call the woman out—He called her up. He did not shame her—He invited her into freedom.

That is what we are called to do. We do not have to judge others to encourage them to live in truth. We do not have to condemn to call people higher. We lead by example. We speak truth in love. We lift, we encourage, we build.

Because when we release judgment, we make room for grace.

SPEAK THIS OUT LOUD:

God, I surrender my plans, my comfort, and my timing to You. I refuse to let fear, doubt, or hesitation hold me back from full obedience. I trust that Your way is better than mine. I declare that I will move when You say move, speak when You say speak, and act when You call me to act. I will not delay, question, or resist Your direction—I will respond with faith and courage. My obedience is not based on my feelings; it is based on my faith. I know that every breakthrough, every blessing, and every next-level opportunity is on the other side of my obedience. I choose to be strong and courageous, to follow Your voice boldly, and to trust that You will meet me every step of the way.

ACTIVATE YOUR IMPACT

DECLARE YOUR OBEDIENCE IS ACTIVATED

I DECLARE I am a person of radical obedience. I will trust God's voice and take action in faith, even when it doesn't make sense!

I DECLARE I will not shrink back in fear. God's plans for my life are greater than my comfort, and I will step forward in boldness!

I DECLARE I serve an audience of One. I am not here to please people—I am here to glorify God with my life and leadership!

I DECLARE my obedience leads to supernatural favor. I trust that when I align my actions with God's will, doors will open that no one can shut!

I DECLARE I will steward my obedience well! I will not hesitate, second-guess, or delay what God has called me to do—I will respond with full faith and trust!

LOL ACTIVATION

Obedience is the bridge between where you are and where God is calling you to be. Every breakthrough, every moment of favor, and every divine connection is unlocked when you choose to obey fully, completely, and without hesitation.

Your obedience determines your impact.

Your impact determines your legacy.

And your legacy determines how the Kingdom of God is expanded through you.

The truth is, obedience is not always easy. It will stretch you, challenge you, and push you beyond your comfort zone. But on the other side of obedience is transformation—your own and the lives of those you are called to impact.

So let's do this. With unwavering faith, full surrender, and a commitment to trust God's plan above your own, answer the following questions:

LEARN IT:

Where have you hesitated in obedience? What has God been asking you to do that you have delayed or resisted?

ACTIVATE YOUR IMPACT

OWN IT:

What area of your life is God calling you to fully surrender? What step of obedience have you been afraid to take?

LIVE IT:

If you committed to full obedience today—without fear, without hesitation—what would change? What is one action step you will take right now to walk in obedience?

Now take a deep breath and declare: *I trust, I obey, I move.* Because when you activate your obedience, you activate your destiny.

Chapter Twelve

ACTIVATE YOUR WORSHIP

Worship changes everything. It shifts the atmosphere. It drowns out the noise. It activates a deeper connection to God.

For me, worship has become a non-negotiable part of my life, my business, and the *Live Out Loud* movement. Worship music, lyrics, and songs have been a catalyst for my faith, my surrender, and my ability to fully receive everything the Holy Spirit has for me. It's how I align my heart with His. It's how I let go of fear. It's how I activate the presence of God in every space I walk into.

But I wasn't always comfortable with it.

There was a time when worship felt intimidating. I remember the first time I saw people raising their hands in worship, praying out loud, fully abandoned in their praise. It made me uncomfortable because I didn't understand it. But here's what I've learned: the enemy uses discomfort to keep us from fully receiving what God has for us.

Worship is meant to be an activation. It's a weapon. It's a release. And when we step into it fully—when we remove the fear, the self-consciousness, and the resistance—it unlocks breakthrough.

WORSHIP IS AN INVITATION TO MORE

One of the most powerful things I've learned is that **worship is a posture of the heart.** It's not about performing. It's not about asking. It's about loving God with everything—our heart, soul, mind, and strength. It's about moving the heart of the Father with our praise.

The Bible is filled with moments where worship shifted everything. Walls fell. Chains broke. Victories were won. Worship wasn't just an afterthought—it was a strategy. And it still is.

I feel music and lyrics deep in my soul. Every worship song that moves me connects to a scripture that I love. That's why I honor and respect worship leaders, songwriters, and those who create anthems that bring heaven to earth. In fact, before I ever wrote this book, I co-wrote a worship song.

WHEN WORSHIP CAME BEFORE THE BOOK

For years, people asked me, *Brooke, when are you going to write your book?* And for years, I struggled to make it happen. I got stuck in the process, pushed it to the side, and put other things in front of it.

But then, something unexpected happened. I was having a conversation with one of my favorite worship singers, sharing how much worship meant to me and how I dreamed of a *Live Out Loud* worship song. And instead of just dreaming about it, she looked at me and said, "Let's write one together."

We talked about the heart of the *Live Out Loud* community. We wrote lyrics that embodied the movement. And before I had a book, I had a song.

ACTIVATE YOUR IMPACT

Live Out Loud

by Meredith Andrews and Brooke Thomas
© 2022 Curb | Word Entertainment

I cancel every lie
That has echoed in my life
Every word that came against
What Heaven says
I silence every doubt
That was meant to take me out
There is nothing that can steal
Your promises

I'm gonna live, gonna live out loud
No shame gonna hold me down
I'm free and chosen, healed and found
Ain't no fear that can stop me now
I'm gonna fight, gonna stand my ground
No chain gonna keep me bound
Loved more ways than I can count
Ain't no fear that can stop me now

My identity redeemed
My tomorrow is secure
I refuse to see through
Anything but faith
If there's power in a sound
Then my heart is gonna roar
With a fire and a force that
Can't be tamed

I'm gonna live, gonna live out loud
No shame gonna hold me down
Free and chosen, healed and found
Ain't no fear that can stop me now
I'm gonna fight, gonna stand my ground
No chain gonna keep me bound
Loved more ways than I can count
Ain't no fear that can stop me now

This is where dry bones get back up again
I prophesy
This is where dead dreams come to life again
I prophesy
This is where faith can change reality
I testify
This is where You redeem my legacy
This is where dry bones get back up again
This is where dead dreams come to life again
This is where faith can change reality
This is where You redeem my legacy

That song meant so much to me because, in a season where I felt inadequate about not finishing my book, I was able to create something that set people free. Women in our community played it on repeat. It got into their spirits. It became an anthem for our movement. And through that process, I realized that creativity flows when we worship first.

That song showed me what I was capable of. It reminded me that worship activates purpose. It unlocks new levels. And it opens the door for God to do what only He can do.

Now you're holding both the book and the song! This proves that anything is possible. If I can do it, you can too!

WORSHIP SETS THE ATMOSPHERE FOR BREAKTHROUGHS

Before I walk into any room—whether it's a stage, a retreat, or a business meeting—I know that the atmosphere matters. And worship? It changes everything.

There are moments when intimidation creeps in. When doubt tries to take up space. When the weight of expectations feels heavy. But when worship is present, fear has no place.

That's why I make it a priority. At my retreats, we start every morning with worship. On my business Zoom calls, we play worship music before diving into strategy. And at encounter nights? We create space for the Holy Spirit to move, for women to let go of fear and step into freedom.

I've seen it firsthand. Women weeping, releasing burdens, stepping into healing, and experiencing the tangible presence of God.

One woman looked at me in the middle of worship and said, "Is this real? What is happening? I feel so free."

I looked back at her and said, "This is the way it's supposed to be."

Because when the Holy Spirit moves, nothing stays the same. Worship sets the table for Him to show up and do what only He can do.

WORSHIP IS A WEAPON AGAINST WORRY

I've learned that worship drowns out worry.

Instead of sitting in anxiety, I choose to praise first. I go into prayer already thanking God for what has been done. If He put something in my heart, I don't beg for it—I thank Him in advance for already making a way.

Worship is how we claim victory over our emotions. It's how we step into alignment with the fruit of the Spirit—love, joy, peace, patience, kindness, goodness, faithfulness, gentleness, and self-control. It's how we silence fear and step boldly into faith.

The Holy Spirit speaks to us in worship. There is no barrier, no restriction—we have access. We can call on Jesus' name, and He will show up. Worship invites breakthrough. It invites healing. It invites freedom.

WORSHIP ALIGNS US WITH HEAVEN

At my events, I often challenge women: *If the world has spaces for silence, for emptying minds, for centering thoughts—why wouldn't we, as believers, create spaces to worship the One who created us?*

We don't need to overcomplicate it. We don't need a perfect setting. Worship is as simple as turning on a song, lifting our hands, and asking the Holy Spirit to invade our hearts.

When we do that, everything shifts. Worry loses its grip. Clarity comes. Breakthrough happens.

The Bible says in Ephesians 1:17-18 that the eyes of our hearts may be enlightened. Worship does that—it opens our spiritual eyes, helps us see clearly, and reminds us of who we are and who God has called us to be.

Every day, we have a choice. To let distractions pull us out of alignment—or to let worship bring us back. To carry the weight of the world—or to lay it down in surrender.

ACTIVATE YOUR IMPACT

Worship is a way to keep our minds, hearts, and spirits focused on God's will, His heart, and His power. It's a posture of obedience, of surrender, and of receiving everything He has for us.

So, wherever you are right now—pause. Turn on a worship song. Lift your hands. And invite God to meet you there.

I promise, He will.

ACTIVATION 1: JOYFUL MEDICINE

> *"A cheerful heart is good medicine, but a crushed spirit dries up the bones."*
> **(Proverbs 17:22, NIV)**

Worship drowns out worry.

I want to teach you how to activate the healing power of joy in your life! Even if that means laughing at yourself sometimes. God designed us for joy—He wired us for it. And a cheerful heart is part of our healing and wholeness.

I keep this verse plastered everywhere as a personal reminder. As high-impact women, we're always in go mode, and so many things can try to break our spirits. Disappointments, rejection, pressure, fear. And when our spirits are crushed, our passion starts to flicker out.

Hope is oxygen for the soul. When we lose our joy, hopelessness sneaks in.

That's why I want to encourage you today to prioritize balance. Yes, you have responsibilities and ambitious goals to accomplish. But you also need to make room for fun. For rest. For deep belly laughs. For the kind of joy that revives your spirit and reminds you who you are in Christ.

If we are not emotionally balanced, everything else in our lives gets thrown off too. That's why Jesus gave us the Sabbath

—not as a rule, but as a gift. We need moments to refresh, recharge, and refocus.

Every action we take and everything we consume affects our confidence. And confidence fuels bold action. When we feel joyful, we show up differently. But when joy is absent, it's easy to shrink back, hide, or stand still.

So what brings you joy? What makes you laugh? What lifts your heart when the weight of the world tries to press down? Lean into those things. Let them be a form of worship, because joy is medicine for the soul.

ACTIVATION 2: LOVE FEST

"God showed how much he loved us by sending his one and only Son into the world so that we might have eternal life through him. This is real love—not that we loved God, but that he loved us and sent his Son as a sacrifice to take away our sins."
(1 John 4:9–10, NLT)

God just wants to be with you.

You were made to be fully loved. Your Heavenly Father sees you, knows you, and values you. But I know there are moments when it does not feel like that is true. Moments when you feel overlooked. When no one seems to notice how hard things actually are. When you wonder if God's love is for everyone else—but maybe not for you.

Those are the exact moments you have a powerful choice. You can choose to have a love fest with your Creator.

Worship is one of the most powerful ways to activate His love in your life. It shifts everything. It moves the Father's heart. It breaks heaviness. It drowns out fear. And it reminds you that you are fully seen, fully known, and fully loved.

I incorporate worship into every aspect of my business

because I have seen what happens when women step into God's presence. Whether at a high-level mastermind, a group coaching session, or an in-person event, everything changes when we start from a place of surrender.

That's when God's love floods in. That's when breakthroughs happen. That's when women unlock new levels of confidence, vision, and purpose.

My pastor once said, "The devil's greatest desire is to take your worship. God's greatest desire is to love you."

So what if today, instead of sitting in doubt, discouragement, or heaviness, you chose to worship? What if you started your own love fest with God, right where you are?

ACTIVATION 3: WHAT NEEDS TO BE REDEEMED OR RESTORED?

"... for in God's presence he believed that God can raise the dead and call into being things that don't even exist yet."
(Romans 4:17, TPT)

Picture Lazarus, his lifeless body wrapped in burial clothes. Lying in a dark tomb for four days. Everyone thought his story was over.

But then Jesus spoke. *"Lazarus, come out!"*

And life came rushing back.

This is the God we serve—a God who specializes in redemption, restoration, and resurrection. Romans 4:17 says He can breathe life into anything that appears dead. He can call into being things that do not even exist yet.

So let me ask: What in your life needs His reviving touch?

What feels lost that God is urging you to reclaim?

What "dead" dreams, relationships, or opportunities is He calling back to life?

I have seen this firsthand with the women in my mastermind groups. I have watched them rise from despair into boldness, from defeat into purpose, and from struggle into breakthrough. Redemption and restoration are part of your inheritance as a daughter of God.

You are not a bystander to brokenness. You are an ambassador of redemption.

You are not stuck in loss. You are stepping into restoration.

God's power is at work in your life. So today, open your hands, lift your eyes, and claim what is being brought back to life.

ACTIVATION 4: REJOICE, EVEN IF...

"Rejoice in the Lord always: and again I say, Rejoice."
(Philippians 4:4, KJV)

Ever felt like you were in the waiting room of life, wondering when it would finally be your turn for a breakthrough?

What if the key to unlocking that breakthrough was simple?

Rejoice.

Even if ... you do not see the change yet.

Even if ... the promise has not come to pass.

Even if ... the circumstances are still uncertain.

I hear this all the time in my coaching sessions: "What if my due season doesn't come tonight, or tomorrow, or even next week?"

And my answer is always the same: Keep trusting God.

You have tried everything else, right? You might as well go all in on the God card. You have nothing to lose and everything to gain.

The truth is, Philippians 4:4 is not just a feel-good verse. Paul is not writing a "good vibes" post for social media.

He says, "Rejoice in the Lord always." Not sometimes. Not when things are easy. Always.

And just in case we missed it, he repeats himself.

Rejoice.

And here's something powerful—"rejoice" does not just mean to feel happy. It literally means to brighten up, to spin around, to leap for joy.

So when you feel pressure, when you feel the weight of waiting, when the enemy whispers doubt in your ear—that is your cue.

Rejoice.

Smile. Spin around. Jump. Lift your hands in victory. Declare Jesus' goodness. Because even if you do not see it yet, the breakthrough is already on its way.

SPEAK THIS OUT LOUD:

God, I give You my worship. I refuse to let fear, distraction, or self-consciousness keep me from fully stepping into Your presence. I declare that worship is my weapon, my breakthrough, and my connection to You. When I lift my voice in praise, the atmosphere shifts, chains break, and miracles happen. I will not be silent. I will not shrink back. I will boldly declare Your goodness, knowing that worship aligns me with Heaven's power. No matter my circumstances, I will rejoice. No matter the waiting, I will praise. No matter the battle, I will worship my way through. Because I know that in Your presence, everything changes.

DECLARE YOUR WORSHIP IS ACTIVATED

I DECLARE worship is my breakthrough. When I praise, strongholds fall, and the atmosphere shifts in my favor!
I DECLARE I will not hold back in worship. I refuse to let fear, doubt, or self-consciousness keep me from fully stepping into God's presence!
I DECLARE my worship silences the enemy. No lie, no fear, no attack can stand against the power of my praise!
I DECLARE worship will be my first response. Before I worry, before I fear, before I overthink—I will lift my voice in praise and trust God completely!

I am aligned with Heaven, fully surrendered, and ready to receive all that God has for me!

LOL ACTIVATION

Worship is not a ritual—it is a weapon. It is an invitation. It is a posture that shifts everything in your life.

What you worship determines what you magnify.

What you magnify determines what you focus on.

And what you focus on determines what grows in your life.

When you worship, you invite Heaven to invade your circumstances. You remove fear's grip. You set the stage for miracles.

So let's do this. With an open heart, full surrender, and a commitment to activate the power of worship in your life, answer the following questions:

LEARN IT:

Where have you resisted worship? Where have you let distractions, discomfort, or self-consciousness keep you from fully entering into God's presence?

OWN IT:

How can you make worship a non-negotiable part of your daily life? What shift will you make to put praise before worry?

LIVE IT:

If you fully activated the power of worship today—without holding back, without overthinking—what would change? What is one action step you will take right now to step into deeper worship?

Now, take a deep breath and declare: *I worship, I surrender, I receive.* Because when you activate your worship, you activate your victory.

Conclusion

THE ACTIVATION IS YOURS

I pray this book becomes a lifelong tool for you—a place you return to when you need to be reminded, reignited, and reactivated in your faith, business, and purpose.

But here's the truth: the activation was never in these pages alone. It was in you all along.

You have always carried the potential, the power, and the authority to walk boldly in your calling. What we've done together in these pages is *unlock* what was already placed inside of you. You have been chosen, set apart, and equipped for such a time as this.

So, what happens next?

The journey doesn't end here. Activation is a daily decision. It's waking up every morning and saying, *"God, I trust You. I'm ready to walk in obedience. I'm ready to lead boldly and live fully."*

It's choosing to show up—when it's exciting and when it's challenging. It's moving forward when doors fly open and when obstacles try to block your path. It's standing firm when doubt creeps in and others don't understand the assignment God has given you.

Because here's the truth: you are not the same woman who started this book. You are awake. You are activated. And you are ready to take a leap of faith.

There will still be moments of uncertainty, but you now hold the keys to unlock boldness and breakthrough in every area of your life.

WHAT WILL YOU DO WITH THIS ACTIVATION?

Now that you know what's possible, you have a choice.

You can return to comfort, staying where it feels safe … or you can step into everything God has called you to.

I already know which one you're going to choose. You are not a woman who stays stuck. You are a builder. A creator. A leader. A trailblazer.

You are called to shift atmospheres. To build a business that reflects Kingdom excellence. To live a life of impact and influence. To walk in unwavering faith.

Here's the best part: You're not doing it alone. God has gone before you, making a way where there seemed to be none. He is ordering your steps, orchestrating divine connections, and preparing doors that only He can open.

And if you ever feel resistance along the way? If doubt tries to whisper that you're not enough? If the enemy attempts to distract, discourage, or derail you?

Remember who you are.

You are a daughter of the King. Chosen. Set apart. Covered in His strength. Backed by His power. Empowered by His Spirit.

Nothing can stop you.

NO EXCUSES!

Let me ask you: "Are you *waiting* for something to change?"

Are you waiting for the perfect moment to launch, expand,

hire, or step into the next level of your business? Are you waiting for a sign, for someone to validate you, for circumstances to align just right?

Because if that's the case, I want you to hear this loud and clear: You don't have to wait any longer.

In the book of John, a man had been stuck for 38 years—waiting for something outside of himself to change before he could move forward. Then Jesus walked up to him and asked a direct question: *"Do you want to be made well?"*

The man immediately started listing reasons why it wasn't possible.

Jesus didn't accept the excuses.

Instead, He gave him three commands—ones that still hold true for us today:

1. **Get up now!** (Take ownership—your next level isn't coming from someone else handing it to you.)
2. **Roll up your bed.** (Stop holding onto old limitations—you don't need them anymore.)
3. **Walk—and keep walking.** (Move. Take action. Step forward into the thing you've been delaying.)

This is your moment to get up.

This is your moment to stop waiting for the *right* time, the *right* conditions, the *right* opportunity, and realize that everything you need is already inside you.

It's time to stop hesitating. To stop letting doubt, past disappointments, or outside opinions dictate your next move.

You are equipped. You are called. And you already have *permission* to step into everything God has prepared for you.

No more waiting. No more excuses.

The activation is already in you.

So the only question that remains is: Will you choose wisely?

LIVE FULLY ACTIVATED

I am so grateful for you. Thank you for allowing me to speak into your life. Thank you for saying *yes* to your calling.

The world needs what only *you* can bring.

You don't have to do this alone. The *Live Out Loud* community is where activation turns into momentum—where bold, faith-driven women lift each other up, stay obedient to God's calling, and walk out their purpose with confidence.

If you're ready for more support, encouragement, and high-level sisterhood, scan the QR code to step in and see what's possible!

> **Ready to go deeper? Scan the QR code to explore Brooke's latest programs, events, and opportunities to activate your impact and walk boldly in your Kingdom calling.**

No matter what, I want you to remember this: The best is yet to come.

Now go and *activate your impact*!

xo, Brooke

WANT MORE?

*I*f this book activated something inside of you, there's more where that came from. Brooke created *Live Out Loud* to be more than a brand—it's a global community of women living on purpose, walking in obedience, and building the Kingdom of God through business, leadership, and bold faith.

Explore Brooke's Programs:

- **Ignite**—For women ready to activate their faith and build a solid foundation in business.

- **The Live Out Loud Elite Mastermind**—For high-achieving entrepreneurs scaling to 7 figures God's way.

- **The Queen's Table**—An intimate mastermind for faith-driven founders and CEOs of seven to 10-figure businesses building legacy with excellence.

Learn more at www.brookethomas.com.

CONNECT WITH BROOKE

Keep the activation going.

- **Website:** *www.brookethomas.com*

- **Podcast:** *The Live Out Loud Show* (available on all major platforms)

- **Instagram:** *@liveoutloudbrooke*

- **YouTube:** *Brooke Thomas*

- **Email:** support@brookethomas.com

PARTNER IN IMPACT

Want to link arms with other faith-filled women building something bigger than themselves? **Love Out Loud** is Brooke's nonprofit initiative that unites women to give generously, serve boldly, and fund Kingdom missions together.

Learn more at www.loveoutloudgiving.org.

FINAL BLESSING

"Now all glory to God, who is able, through His mighty power at work within us, to do infinitely more than we might ask or think."
(Ephesians 3:20)

ACKNOWLEDGMENTS

First and foremost, I want to give all the glory to God, my Savior, the one who will never fail. This book would not exist without His guidance through every word. His grace, wisdom, and unwavering presence have shaped not only these pages but my entire journey. My biggest goal is to honor God through this book and to be a carrier of His Glory.

To my incredible husband, Brett—thank you for always being my rock. Your constant support, encouragement, and belief in me, especially through the long hours it took to bring this book to life, mean more than you'll ever know. I'm so grateful to walk through life with you. You are my very best friend and biggest cheerleader!

To my beautiful daughters—you are my greatest inspiration. I thought of you and your generation of girls every single day as I worked on this book. Your love, strength, kindness, and faith push me to keep going, to dream bigger, and to live louder.

To one of my very best friends and my business brother Brodie, who has become part of our family—you have always encouraged me, inspired me, and spent countless hours cheering me on. I can't thank you enough for being such a strategic partner with Brett and me!

To my besties, Gilda, Katie, Sara, Corrie-Beth, Heather, and the *Live Out Loud Elite Mastermind* ladies that have become some of my closest friends and prayer warriors—thank you for being my support system throughout this journey. Your encouraging texts and prayers kept me going when it felt like too much. Your wisdom, feedback, and honest input, whether helping me make decisions about the cover or sharing insights that shaped this book, were invaluable. I am beyond blessed to have you in my corner, cheering me on every step of the way.

To my *Queen's Table* ladies—leading the way and showing the world what is possible. You are the women paving the way as pioneers with boldness and faith. I am honored by your trust —not just in me, but in the calling God has placed on your lives. You have also become some of my closest friends in my inner circle, and I am forever grateful for the front-row seat I have to watch you live fully awake and activated in your impact. Thank you for your brave example that inspired me in my dream to create this book.

To the women of the *Live Out Loud* community—you are the heartbeat of this book. I am incredibly thankful for those of you who so bravely shared your stories within these pages. I am also thankful for the thousands of other women whose breakthroughs, boldness, and faith-filled pursuit of their God-given purpose inspire me every single day. Leading you is one of my greatest honors in this life.

To the *Live Out Loud* team—For the weekends and late nights you spent helping me shape these pages. Thank you for relentlessly championing this mission. Your dedication and belief in the vision make everything we do possible. I am especially grateful to my Marketing Director, Amanda Mick, whose tireless work and unwavering commitment made this book launch a reality—all while being nine months pregnant. You are a true warrior.

To my incredible pastors, Mark and Rachelle Francey—thank you for continually pouring into me and helping me grow deeper in my faith. Your leadership and teaching strengthen my spirit and fuel the fire that keeps me going.

To my mentors—thank you for calling me higher, and reminding me of the responsibility we carry as Kingdom leaders. Your wisdom, honesty, and belief in my calling have been a priceless gift.

To you, the reader—whether we've met before or this is the first time our paths have crossed, I want you to know this: you were on my heart as I wrote these words. My prayer is that this book activates something new and powerful in you—that it stirs your spirit, strengthens your faith, and awakens you to the extraordinary impact God has placed inside of you.

To my publisher and team at Game Changing Publishing—thank you for believing in this book and what it could be. Your dedication, expertise, and passion helped bring this vision to life, and I am so grateful for your partnership.

And to everyone who ever asked me about writing a book—thank you for seeing something in me that I hadn't yet fully embraced. It would have taken me 10 more years to put these words on paper were it not for the amazing women around me who kept saying, "It's time." You pushed me to be obedient to the calling, and I am forever grateful.

Thank you for being a part of this journey. Let's go boldly together—fully alive, fully activated, and fully surrendered to the calling God has placed on our lives.

With love and gratitude,
Brooke Thomas

ABOUT BROOKE THOMAS

Brooke Thomas is a powerhouse business mentor, speaker, podcast host, and founder of *Live Out Loud*, a multimillion-dollar personal development brand rooted in faith, bold leadership, and Kingdom impact.

For more than two decades, Brooke has built and scaled multiple seven-figure businesses. Now she empowers other women to do the same with strategies and confidence that are aligned with who God created her to be.

Brooke is also a stage 3 melanoma survivor and has been cancer-free for nearly two decades. After defying a devastating prognosis during her first pregnancy, Brooke uses her story to inspire others to live fully awake and pursue their God-sized dreams.

In addition to creating transformative live events, retreats, masterminds, and coaching memberships, Brooke holds a degree in Business Administration. She began her career in corporate sales, but it didn't take her long to realize she had the heart of an entrepreneur. She has risen to the top of two successful network marketing companies. Today, she leads an organization of more than 320,000 business partners worldwide, mentoring women on building residual income with both excellence and integrity.

Brooke has been featured in *Forbes*, *Huffington Post*, and *InStyle Magazine*, and has appeared as an expert on NBC, CBS, and multiple other networks. She is also the host of *The Live Out Loud Show*, a top-rated podcast designed to ignite clarity, confidence, and courage for women in their business, life, and faith.

She is also the founder of Love Out Loud, a nonprofit that unites faith-based women in business to pool their resources and increase their impact for Kingdom causes.

Brooke has been married to her husband, Brett, for 21 years. They live in Newport Beach, California, with their two beautiful daughters. Her life and business are a testament to what happens when you stop living by the world's rules and start living by God's truth.

She doesn't just teach strategy—she leads with spirit. She doesn't just talk about impact—she activates it. And now, she's inviting you to do the same!

Made in United States
Orlando, FL
17 April 2025